Professional Writing Skills

A Self-Paced Training Program

by Janis Fisher Chan
and Diane Lutovich

Advanced Communication Designs, Inc.
P.O. Box 2504, San Anselmo, CA 94979
Phone (415) 459-3563 Fax (415) 459-8618
Email: adcom@linex.com On the Web: www.writeitwell.com

© Advanced Communication Designs, Inc.
2nd edition, 1997, revised 1999
ISBN 0-9637455-4-9

CONTENTS

INTRODUCTION

INTRODUCTION

ABOUT THIS PROGRAM

You're about to begin a writing skills program that will help you write more clearly, effectively and easily. The program has six lessons, each covering a different writing topic.

In Lessons 1, 2 and 3, you'll learn a step-by-step process for planning and writing clear, concise Email messages, memos, letters, reports, proposals, marketing materials, informational documents, and more.

In Lessons 4, 5 and 6, you'll review principles of clear language, grammar and punctuation.

In each lesson, you'll complete practice exercises and writing assignments which help you learn the techniques and apply them to your own writing. The more attention you pay to the exercises and assignments, the more you'll get out of the program.

This program takes about six to ten hours to complete. Before you begin, take a few moments to think about why you want to improve your writing and what you hope to accomplish.

ABOUT YOUR WRITING

What kinds of documents do you write? Letters to customers and vendors? Reports to clients and managers? Memos to team members and others in your organization? Requests for information and action? Press releases? Product descriptions?

Think about the writing you do on the job. What might happen if you . . .

- are misunderstood?
- leave something out?
- fail to get the main point across?
- convey the wrong tone?
- use confusing or unnecessary words?
- use incorrect grammar, punctuation or spelling?

If you are misunderstood, leave something out or fail to get the main point across, readers might take the wrong action or no action at all. The wrong tone might offend a client. Confusing or unnecessary words force readers to work too hard to get the message. And errors in grammar, punctuation or spelling convey a negative image of you and your organization.

ABOUT YOUR OBJECTIVES

Why are you taking this program? On the checklist below, mark the statements that express what you would like to be able to do when you finish the program:

- ☐ get started more easily
- ☐ say what I mean to say
- ☐ get results from my writing
- ☐ get to the point quickly
- ☐ know what information to include
- ☐ organize information logically
- ☐ write more quickly
- ☐ write effective openings and closings
- ☐ use the right tone
- ☐ know when to start a new paragraph
- ☐ use fewer words
- ☐ use clear, concise language
- ☐ use the right grammar, sentence structure and punctuation
- ☐ other

_____

The statements you checked are your **objectives**. Put a ✓ next to the three that are most important to you.

PROGRAM OBJECTIVES

When you complete this program, you will be able to write more effectively and easily by:

PLANNING YOUR WRITING   LESSON 1

In this lesson, you'll learn the first three planning steps:

■ Look at your message from your reader's point of view

■ Decide what you want to accomplish — whether to influence your readers to do something or inform them about something

■ Compose a key sentence that expresses your most important message

DECIDING WHAT INFORMATION TO INCLUDE AND ORGANIZING IT LOGICALLY   LESSON 2

In this lesson, you'll learn to:

■ Select the information to include

■ Organize information logically

WRITING A ROUGH DRAFT   LESSON 3

In this lesson, you'll learn to write a first draft by:

■ Reviewing your writing plan and revising it as needed to make sure it is sound

■ Writing an opening that catches readers' attention and clearly says what you are writing about

■ Using transitions to link points, paragraphs and sections smoothly

■ Using lists to present information so readers can grasp it quickly

■ Writing a closing that sums up points as needed and tells readers clearly what happens next

USING LANGUAGE THAT COMMUNICATES CLEARLY LESSON 4

In this lesson, you'll learn to use:

- Active language
- Specific words
- Plain English
- Real words

USING CONCISE LANGUAGE LESSON 5

In this lesson, you'll learn to write more concisely by:

- Identifying and eliminating unnecessary words

USING CORRECT SENTENCE STRUCTURE, LESSON 6
PUNCTUATION AND GRAMMAR

In this lesson, you'll learn to write clearly and professionally by:

- Using correct sentence structure, punctuation and grammar

BEFORE YOU BEGIN

During each lesson, you will complete practice exercises and writing assignments that help you apply what you're learning.

From time to time, you will be asked to review, evaluate and/or revise your own writing. So before you begin Lesson 1, *collect three samples of your writing*—memos, letters, Email messages, reports and/or proposals. If possible, find samples of writing you've done within the last six months.

Keep the samples handy. You will refer to them throughout the program.

SCHEDULING YOUR TIME

"Self-paced" instruction means just that—you work at your own pace.

Depending on how fast you like to work, you can plan on spending from six to ten hours on this program. Except for the Overview, which takes about half an hour to complete, each lesson takes from one to two hours. Try to allow enough time to complete a lesson in one session.

Give yourself a deadline for completing the program. It's best to complete the entire program within four weeks.

When you're ready, turn to the Overview, where you will examine the purpose of business and professional writing and develop criteria for effective writing.

OVERVIEW

OVERVIEW

The Purpose of Business and Professional Writing

Business writing is unique. It is distinguished from other types of writing by its content, its form and its purpose.

For example:

■ The purpose of fiction is to create a world, based on reality or not, in which readers can experience such feelings as fear, amusement, loneliness, suspense, joy, and adventure.

> The great Pullman was whirling onward with such dignity of motion that a glance from the window seemed simply to prove that the plains of Texas were pouring eastward. Vast flats of green grass, dull-hued spaces of mesquite and cactus, groups of frame houses, woods of light and tender trees, all were sweeping into the east over the horizon, a precipice.
>
> "The Bride Comes to Yellow Sky"
> Stephen Crane

■ The purpose of an essay is to analyze or interpret a situation, usually from a personal point of view.

> A few years ago I wrote a book which dealt in part with the difficulties of the English in India. Feeling that they would have had no difficulties in India themselves, the Americans read the book freely. The more they read it the better it made them feel, and a cheque to the author was the result. I bought a wood with the cheque. It is not a large wood—it contains scarcely any trees, and it is intersected, blast it, by a public footpath. Still, it is the first property that I have owned, so it is right that other people should participate in my shame, and should ask themselves, in accents that will vary in horror, this very important question: What is the effect of property upon the character?
>
> "My Wood"
> E. M. Forster

■ The purpose of personal writing is to express personal experiences, needs, feelings, and expectations.

```
Dear Mother,

I'm sorry I forgot your birthday. October came
so fast this year — I hadn't even realized
summer was over. I hope it was a happy day, and
that you were not too hurt when I didn't call.

                              Love,
                              Your son
```

But what is the purpose of business writing? Read this Email message. Then briefly describe its purpose.

```
TO:        Data Processing Managers
RE:        Data Processing delays

The Data Processing group has failed to meet its
deadlines for the past several months. This failure
is causing delays and confusion throughout the
organization. As a manager, you can do two things
to help solve the problem:

•  Make sure your team members are familiar with
   the Data Processing Organizational Format. By
   reading and following the plan, they should be
   able to avoid duplicating each other's efforts.
   The Format also explains each member's
   responsibilities so any one person can fill in
   for another when needed.

•  When reporting any problems, follow the
   procedures clearly established on page 603 of
   the Manager's Handbook.

If you have questions or other suggestions, please
call.
```

The purpose of business writing is _____

_____

_____

Compare your response to the one on the next page.

Business and professional writing helps people conduct business by providing them with information they need.

To accomplish its purpose, business writing *must* be easy to understand. In fact, the best way to determine whether a business document is well written is to take the reader's point of view. Try that now.

Imagine you are one of the staff members to whom this memo is addressed. Read the memo. Then answer the questions on the facing page.

TO: All Document Control Staff

FROM: Department Manager

SUBJECT: Policy on Social Visits During Working Hours

Due to the location of Document Control, we have a great number of people from other departments who come into our department. We have tried to minimize the disruption within our department by implementing a plan to position the print ordering and pick-up window as close to the stairs as possible. In spite of these efforts, we still have a multitude of people coming into the department for strictly social visits. One or two minutes for a social visit is no big deal, but many conversations go on for five minutes or more. If everyone in the department had one visit of five minutes per day the affect would be four hours of lost time per day. We have a high work load and need to be as productive as possible.

It is my recommendation that if anyone initiates a social conversation with you that lasts more than one or two minutes, it should be suggested that you are busy and they should come back at your break or at lunch to continue the conversation.

On a more positive note, I would like to thank each of you for the extra effort that you have expended as a result of the heavy work load. We are very fortunate to be in an industry that is expanding. FLEC is the leader in our industry, we are the largest manufacturer of helix type FRT's in the world. There is no reason to be complacent, as the competition is working hard to catch up. We must continue to optimize our opportunities. Again, I want to thank you and keep up the good work.

1. State the writer's main point in one sentence.

   _____

   _____

   ☐ I'm not sure what the writer's main point is.

2. Did you have to re-read the memo to understand what the writer was trying to say?

   ☐ YES   ☐ NO

3. What is your image of the person who wrote this memo?

   _____

   _____

   _____

   _____

   _____

   Turn the page for a discussion of the memo.

1. You may have had difficulty identifying the writer's main point—it's not clearly stated, and what is there is buried in the middle of the memo.

   Here are two possible main points:

   ■ "Keep social visits to a few minutes."

   ■ "Thanks for your extra effort."

2. It would be very difficult to understand this memo without re-reading it, and that's a waste of time. Writers are responsible for presenting information so readers only have to read it once.

3. Whatever your image of this writer, it's probably not the image the person would like to project. The impression is of someone who is disorganized and unfocussed—or who has trouble expressing what he or she wants to say. The writer doesn't seem to have spent much time on the memo, implying that it isn't very important. And if it isn't important, why should you bother reading it?

Suppose you were asked to help this writer. Use the space below to list suggestions you would make to help the person write more clearly. The first one is done for you.

I would tell this writer to:

■ state the main point clearly, right at the beginning

■ _____

■ _____

■ _____

■ _____

CRITERIA FOR EFFECTIVE BUSINESS WRITING

For business writing to be effective, the writer must:

- state the main point clearly, right at the beginning
- organize information logically
- leave out unnecessary information
- use short sentences and paragraphs
- eliminate unnecessary words
- include all necessary information
- use active, precise language and plain English
- use correct grammar, punctuation and spelling

Now you have a list of standards for your writing to meet. During this program, you'll learn to develop business writing that meets those standards.

**You are ready to begin Lesson 1.
If you'd like, take a break first.**

LESSON 1.
DEVELOPING A WRITING PLAN, STEPS 1–3

L E S S O N 1
Developing a Writing Plan, Steps 1–3

Introduction

In the Overview you learned that successful business writing meets specific criteria. In this lesson, you'll learn a step-by-step process that guarantees your writing meets those criteria. By following this process, you develop a plan for writing an effective communication.

You would never build a house without blueprints. You also need a plan when you write. A "blueprint" makes it possible to get started easily, decide what information to include and end up with a useful product: a piece of writing your readers can easily and quickly understand.

OBJECTIVES   In this lesson, you'll learn the first three steps for developing a writing plan:

- Look at your message from your reader's point of view

- Decide what you want to accomplish — whether to **influence** your readers to do something or **inform** them about something

- Compose a key sentence that expresses your most important message

WHAT YOU NEED
- a writing tablet

- a pen or pencil

- two or three samples of your writing

In Lessons 1 and 2 of this program, you'll learn a **6-STEP PROCESS** to help you plan your writing logically and efficiently. Each step is carefully designed to move you toward a finished product that says what you want it to say.

Here are the steps:

---

1. LOOK AT WHAT YOU'RE GOING TO WRITE FROM YOUR READER'S POINT OF VIEW.

2. DECIDE WHAT YOU WANT TO ACCOMPLISH: IS YOUR *PRIMARY* PURPOSE TO INFLUENCE READERS OR TO INFORM THEM?

3. COMPOSE A KEY SENTENCE THAT EXPRESSES YOUR MOST IMPORTANT MESSAGE.

4. LIST THE FACTS AND IDEAS THAT WILL ACCOMPLISH YOUR PURPOSE.

5. GROUP POINTS INTO CATEGORIES.

6. WRITE A SUMMARY SENTENCE FOR EACH CATEGORY AND LIST THE SENTENCES IN ORDER.

In this lesson, you'll learn and practice steps 1, 2 and 3.

In Lesson 2, you'll cover steps 4 – 6.

On the next page, begin Step 1, looking at your writing from your reader's point of view.

STEP 1.   LOOK AT WHAT YOU'RE GOING TO WRITE FROM
                          YOUR READER'S POINT OF VIEW

Communication is a two-way process. It takes place when the message you send has been received — and **understood** — by the person at the other end.

When you're face-to-face with people, it's easy to know when they aren't getting your message. Furrowed eyebrows, a vacant look, restlessness, questions—all are signs that listeners are confused.

Here's a common situation. Jillian has just started an important project. She will need several key pieces of information from Alan, who works in another division of her company. She sends Alan a detailed Email explaining what she needs and when she needs it.

As long as Alan understands her message, he will probably send the information—or at least let her know if he can't.

But what if Jillian's message is confusing? List some ways Jillian might know that Alan did not understand what she meant.

■ _____

■ _____

■ _____

■ _____

■ _____

If Jillian's message is not clear, Alan might send the wrong information or might not respond at all. Or he might have to call Jillian to ask what she meant. Jillian would have wasted valuable time — hers and Alan's.

Writers sometimes fail to communicate clearly because they haven't stopped to consider their readers. Will readers be interested in the information? Do readers know anything about the subject? Will the message make readers uncomfortable? It's important to answer these kinds of questions **before** starting to write.

One of the most important steps you can take to increase the chances of readers getting your message is to look at what you're writing from the **reader's point of view.**

Depending on what you're writing, readers may be very interested in the subject, only slightly interested, or not interested at all. They may agree or disagree with your message. They may accept you as an authority on the subject, or they may not have the slightest idea about how expert you are. They may know as much as you know about the subject, or they may not know anything about it. All these factors can affect their response.

By thinking about your reader's needs and interests, you can usually identify some predictable reactions **before** you start writing. Keeping these reactions in mind, you can try to overcome potential resistance, answer questions readers might have, and even increase your credibility.

TRY IT

Here are some typical writing situations. Check one that is real and current for you.

I am writing to influence my reader to:

☐ adjust my bill

☐ correct a problem

☐ hire more staff

☐ change a procedure

☐ other _____

I am writing to inform my reader about:

☐ a special assignment I have completed

☐ a business conference I attended

☐ the status of a current project

☐ other _____

After you've chosen the situation, write the name of the person who would receive the memo or letter here. (If you have more than one reader, list their names or describe the group: e.g., "my clients.")

READER'S NAME: _____

Now try to get a clear picture of your reader by asking and answering some of the questions listed below. Add others that you think might be important.

IS THE READER . . .

☐ expecting to hear from me?

☐ familiar with this subject?

☐ already interested in what I have to say?

☐ likely to consider me an authority on the subject?

☐ likely to find what I have to say useful?

☐ familiar with my views on this subject?

☐ already committed to a point of view?

☐ likely to agree with my point of view?

☐ likely to find my message uncomfortable or threatening?

☐ other _____

_____

_____

Never skip this step. Remember, you are writing because you need to communicate something specific to another person. To determine what information to include and to convey that information clearly, you must first focus on your **reader.**

❖ **HINT**   What if you don't know your reader? Consider what you know **about** him or her. Is the person a decision-maker? Busy? Likely to receive many letters like yours each week? Does the person need your business? A few educated guesses can help you focus even on readers you've never met.

**Now you've looked at what you're going to write
from your reader's point of view. Next,
you'll look at ways to determine
your purpose for writing.**

STEP 2. DECIDE WHAT YOU WANT TO ACCOMPLISH: IS YOUR *PRIMARY* PURPOSE TO INFLUENCE READERS OR TO INFORM THEM?

To get results, you must clarify exactly what you want to accomplish. Then you will be able to state your most important message clearly.

Your **primary purpose** for writing always falls into one of two categories: to **influence** your reader to do something or to **inform** your reader about something.

Here is a short memo. As you read it, try to decide whether the writer's primary purpose for writing is to influence the reader or to inform her.

TO: Diane Anderson
FROM: Michael Bellows
RE: Annual Sales Conference

I would like you to consider moving this year's sales conference to the Horizons Resort Hotel in Marina.

The Horizons, which has all the facilities we need, has offered us an excellent package (I've enclosed details). Marina is centrally located and is served by all the major airlines. If we sign a contract by January 15, the Horizons will give us an additional five percent discount on room rates.

Let me know if you need more information. I'd like to confirm conference plans by the end of next week.

Michael's **primary** purpose was to **influence** Diane to do something—move the sales conference to the Horizons Resort Hotel in Marina.

Now read this Email message and see if you can tell whether the writer's primary purpose is to **influence** the reader to do something or to **inform** the reader about something.

```
TO:        George Blocker
FROM:      Eileen McGuigo
SUBJECT:   Three-Shift Coverage in Processing

For the last several weeks, we have been provided
with three-shift coverage in the Processing
Department. Company employees have covered the day
shift and swing shift. A temporary employee has been
covering the night shift. The third shift was covered
on a trial basis and is scheduled to end this week.
This has been satisfactory and should be continued.
```

You might have concluded that Eileen's primary purpose was to influence George to keep the temporary worker on the night shift. Perhaps you decided the purpose was to inform George about the way the department has been covered for the last three weeks. Or you may not have been able to identify Eileen's primary purpose.

What would you do if you received that message? You might put it in the trash. It has no sense of urgency and no apparent usefulness.

Here's another version of the message. Now can you identify Eileen's primary purpose?

```
TO:        George Blocker
FROM:      Eileen McGuigo
SUBJECT:   Three-Shift Coverage in Processing

I recommend continuing the three-shift coverage that
has been working so well in the Processing Department.

By having company employees cover the day and swing
shifts and hiring a temporary employee for the night
shift, we have met all our deadlines and made the
most efficient use of employees' time.

Please let me know what you decide.
```

In the second version of the message, you can easily see the writer wants to encourage the reader to continue three-shift coverage in Processing. The primary purpose is right in the first paragraph.

HERE'S AN IMPORTANT REMINDER: You often have more than one purpose when you write. But if the purposes have equal weight, they can end up competing with one another for the reader's attention. It is essential to make one purpose **primary**.

It's a little like taking photographs. When amateurs use a camera, they often try to get everything and everybody in the frame. The result? A confusing picture in which it's hard to see what the photographer found interesting or worthwhile.

A skilled photographer, on the other hand, makes sure that the most important subject dominates the picture. The viewer's eye is drawn to the subject, no matter how many other people or objects are in the frame.

When you write, help the reader focus on the most important point. Do that by determining your **primary** purpose for writing.

Here are some examples:

You write **primarily to INFLUENCE** readers when you write. . .

. . . a memo asking the head office to approve your request for a personal computer

. . . a proposal urging a prospective client to hire your firm for a consulting project

You write **primarily to INFORM** readers when you write. . .

. . . a letter to a client explaining the reasons for cancelling an insurance policy

. . . a report detailing the results of a research project

As you read the examples on the next page, you'll see that if a letter or memo is well written you can easily identify the writer's primary purpose.

Here are two letters on similar subjects. Notice how easy it is to see the writer's purpose in each letter.

EXAMPLE 1. INFLUENCE reader to agree to be the keynote speaker

---

Dear Ms. Layton:

I know you are very busy, but we would be delighted if you would agree to be the Keynote Speaker at the first meeting of Mountain Climbers Anonymous.

Our members would love hearing about your struggles with the obsession to scale great heights. I know your experience and perspectives will be of great value to us.

The meeting will be held on Thursday, October 11, 6:30 p.m., at the Tiptop Cafe. Please let me know by August 31 whether you will be available to speak.

EXAMPLE 2. INFORM readers about the first meeting

Dear Mr. Williams:

The first meeting of Mountain Climbers Anonymous will be held on Thursday, October 11, 6:30 p.m., at the Tiptop Cafe.

Our Keynote Speaker will be Ms. Marybeth Layton who will share with us her own struggle to overcome the obsession to scale great heights.

If you plan to attend, we need your reservation form by September 16 so we can order dinner. We hope to see you at the meeting.

PRACTICE

Read each memo and identify its primary purpose.

Alicia—

I'd like to suggest you prepare and distribute an agenda several days before each monthly meeting.

Without an agenda, people waste time coming to meetings they really don't have to attend. Also, people come unprepared to discuss issues because they don't know in advance what will be covered.

I'll be glad to help in any way I can--just let me know.

PRIMARY PURPOSE: ☐ **INFLUENCE**   ☐ **INFORM**

TO: Planning Committee Members

RE: Monthly Planning Meeting, August 12

Here's the Agenda for our next meeting. I've listed the issues we're discussing so you can come prepared.

If you're not involved in any of the areas on the Agenda, you may skip this meeting, but please call me if you do not plan to attend.

PRIMARY PURPOSE: ☐ **INFLUENCE**   ☐ **INFORM**

Turn the page for the answers.

ANSWERS TO PRACTICE

Alicia—

I'd like to suggest you prepare and distribute an agenda several days before each monthly meeting.

Without an agenda, people waste time coming to meetings they really don't have to attend. Also, people come unprepared to discuss issues because they don't know in advance what will be covered.

I'll be glad to help in any way I can--just let me know.

PRIMARY PURPOSE: ☒ **INFLUENCE**   ☐ **INFORM**

The writer's primary purpose is to **influence** Alicia to prepare and distribute an agenda before the meeting.

TO: Planning Committee Members

RE: Monthly Planning Meeting, August 12

Here's the Agenda for our next meeting. I've listed the issues we're discussing so you can come prepared.

If you're not involved in any of the areas on the Agenda, you may skip this meeting, but please call me if you do not plan to attend.

PRIMARY PURPOSE: ☐ **INFLUENCE**   ☒ **INFORM**

The writer's primary purpose is to **inform** committee members of the Agenda for the meeting.

The purpose is clear in the memos because the writers took the time to decide whether they wanted to **influence** or to **inform** readers.

OPTIONAL PRACTICE

If you have samples of your own writing, take them out now.

Read each sample and decide if your **primary** purpose was to **influence** readers to do something or to **inform** them about something.

Do you think your purpose was clear to your readers? If not, make a mental note to determine your primary purpose the next time you write.

**Now that you know the importance of focusing on your reader
and determining your primary purpose for writing, you're
ready for the next step: composing a sentence
that expresses your most important message.**

STEP 3.   COMPOSE A KEY SENTENCE THAT EXPRESSES
YOUR MOST IMPORTANT MESSAGE

Think of your **key sentence** as the one you'd shout if you had three seconds to get your most important message across to someone driving by.

In a well-written memo, the sentence carrying the most important message should be so clear that the reader can easily identify it.

Which of the memos below has a clear key sentence?

MEMO A

> Dear Ms. Montoya:
>
> As a Marketing Director, you are probably concerned with retaining customer loyalty and attracting new customers.
>
> CommCo Advertising Services has been in business for over 15 years, helping companies like yours. We are well qualified for working with you to identify the best approach to meet your needs.
>
> The enclosed brochure describes our services. Thank you for your consideration.

MEMO B

> Dear Mr. Weller:
>
> Is one of your primary concerns finding effective ways to attract new customers to the Burkhart Company? If so, I would like to meet with you and tell you about the very successful advertising campaigns CommCo has designed to do just that.
>
> For the past 15 years, we have specialized in helping growing companies develop effective marketing strategies that reach increasing numbers of new customers. I know we can do the same for you.
>
> The enclosed brochure describes our services and lists some of our clients. Please let me know if you have questions. Otherwise, I'll call next week to see if you're ready to set up an appointment.

The key sentence in **Memo B** jumps right out, doesn't it? All key sentences should be this easy to find.

Dear Mr. Weller:

Is one of your primary concerns finding effective ways to attract new customers to the Burkhart Company? If so, **I would like to meet with you and tell you about the very successful advertising campaigns CommCo has designed to do just that.**

For the past 15 years, we have specialized in helping growing companies develop effective marketing strategies that reach increasing numbers of new customers. I know we can do the same for you.

The enclosed brochure describes our services and lists some of our clients. Please let me know if you have questions. Otherwise, I'll call next week to see if you're ready to set up an appointment.

But what about Memo A? It appears not to have a key sentence. That memo may not get results.

Writers often fail to include a clear key sentence because they:

■ haven't decided what they want to say

■ hesitate to state their main point directly

But readers are busy people. They don't have time to guess what you meant to say. It is your job to express your most important message clearly. You must be willing to take the time to **compose a clear, complete, key sentence**.

Turn the page for examples of key sentences that tell readers exactly what the writer wants them to do or to know.

Examples of Key Sentences

WRITING TO INFLUENCE

I want my reader to . . .

```
... give me a 20 per cent raise.

... reduce your fee by half.

... build a swimming pool at the new facility.
```

WRITING TO INFORM

I want my reader to know that . . .

```
... the project I'm coordinating will be finished
by May 19.

... I am sorry to tell you that your application
for a loan has been denied.

... the needs assessment we conducted indicates
that two-thirds of your staff would benefit from
writing skills training.
```

Not only is it important to include your most important message, you must express this main point as specifically and directly as possible.

Read these pairs of key sentences. Which version in each pair do you think is more specific and direct?

```
a.  It would be appreciated if payment could be sent
    by June 10.

b.  Please send your payment by June 10.
```

```
a.  Payroll vouchers are needed on Thursday if
    paychecks are desired by Friday.

b.  To get paid on Friday, employees must submit
    their payroll vouchers by Thursday.
```

If you think that "b" in each pair is more specific and direct, you are able to recognize a well-written key sentence.

Turn the page for some practice.

PRACTICE

In each situation below, the writer wants to **influence** the reader to **do something**. For each situation, write a **key sentence** that says clearly what the writer wants the reader to do. Feel free to invent information if you need to.

SITUATION: Employees are parking in the visitor lot instead of the employee lot, taking up all the spaces reserved for clients.

_____

_____

_____

SITUATION: You cancelled your Book Club membership over a year ago, but they keep sending you books. You're getting tired of taking books to the Post Office every month to return them.

_____

_____

_____

**Check your answers
on the next page.**

ANSWERS TO PRACTICE

Your key sentences probably resemble these. If yours are very different, be sure they clearly express what the writer wants the reader to do.

```
TO: All employees

Please park in the employees' lot instead of the
visitors' lot.
```

```
Dear Book Club:

Stop sending me books!
```

Clear key sentences make it much more likely that your writing will get results.

The key sentences you just composed were for situations where the writers want to **influence** readers to do something.

Key sentences read a little differently when your primary purpose is to **inform** readers about something.

Read the examples on the next page. The key sentences are highlighted.

PRIMARY PURPOSE: TO INFORM

TO: Staff
RE: Holiday Party

The Holiday Party will be held on December 16 at the Redwood Lodge, noon to 5:00 p.m.

The sign-up sheet will be posted in the cafeteria by Friday. This year, we're asking everyone to bring a few cans of food for the food drive instead of gifts.

If you have questions, please call Miriam Belladora at Extension 403. We hope you and your family can attend.

Here's another memo to inform. Notice that when you're writing to inform, your "key sentence" might actually be a 1–3 sentence statement, as shown in the example.

PRIMARY PURPOSE: TO INFORM

Dear Clients:

On June 15, I am beginning a three-month leave. While I'm away, my associate, Annabel Leong, will be managing my projects.

Before I leave, Annabel and I will do the following to make sure that everything runs smoothly:

- We will review the status of all projects and meet with the project teams.

- During the last two weeks of May, Annabel will call each of you to introduce herself and answer any questions you might have.

- I will provide Annabel with all the project files so she can answer questions and resolve any problems that might come up.

I've enclosed Annabel's business card. You can reach her by telephone, fax, and Email.

I look forward to working with you again when I return in September.

OPTIONAL PRACTICE

If you have your own writing samples, take them out now. Read each sample and underline your **key sentence**: the one that tells the reader precisely **what to do** or **what to know**.

If you cannot find a key sentence, compose one. Promise yourself to include a clear key sentence the next time you write.

NOTE   If you're writing to inform, keep in mind that your "key sentence" might actually be a 1–3 sentence statement.

❖ **HINT**

You have probably noticed that there is a close relationship between the key sentence and the primary writing purpose. If you have trouble composing a key sentence, ask yourself if you have really decided whether your primary purpose is to **influence** or to **inform**.

Review

You have finished Lesson 1.

Next, you'll apply what you've learned to your own writing. But first, here's a quick review of what you've learned so far.

Write the correct word or phrase in the blanks below. If you're not sure what to write, you'll find the answer on the page in parentheses to the right of the sentence.

To begin a writing plan:

■ look at your message from your _____'s
   point of view   (18)

■ decide on your primary purpose: to _____

   or to _____ readers   (21)

■ compose a _____ _____ that expresses

   your most important _____.   (28)

**On the next page, you'll find an assignment that will help
you apply what you've learned to your own writing.**

ASSIGNMENT

For this assignment, complete the first part of a writing plan for a current writing situation of your own. Follow these steps:

1. Think of an Email message, memo, letter, or short report you need to write. If nothing comes to mind, consider one of these topics:

    ■ convince your lawyer, doctor, accountant, etc. to reduce his or her fees for a specific service or visit

    ■ encourage your manager to make a particular purchase for your department

    ■ suggest a change in the way a procedure is carried out at your place of work

2. Now, remove a **Writing Worksheet** from the back of this book.

    Notice that the Worksheet includes all six steps of the writing process. For this assignment, however, **complete only Steps 1, 2 and 3.** You'll learn about Steps 4, 5 and 6 in the next lesson.

3. When you have finished Steps 1, 2 and 3 on the Worksheet:

    ■ put the Worksheet aside — you'll finish it at the end of Lesson 2

    ■ begin Lesson 2 (take a break first if you'd like)

OPTION   If you prefer, go ahead and finish this piece of writing now and choose another situation for the assignment at the end of Lesson 2.

One caution: If you have trouble writing the draft, you're not happy with the finished product, or the document seems incomplete, the first three planning steps may not have been enough. In that case, you need the steps for selecting and organizing information that you'll find in Lesson 2.

What's Next?

In Lesson 2, you'll learn the next steps in the planning process — the steps for selecting the information to include and organizing it logically.

LESSON 2.
DEVELOPING A WRITING PLAN, STEPS 4–6

L E S S O N   2
Developing a Writing Plan, Steps 4–6

Introduction

In Lesson 1, you learned the first three steps to take when you write: consider your reader's point of view, decide what you want to accomplish, and state your main point clearly.

In this lesson, you'll learn the rest of the planning process: deciding what information to include and organizing information so readers can easily follow your points.

OBJECTIVES   In this lesson, you'll learn to:

■ Select the information to include

■ Organize information logically

WHAT YOU NEED

■ a writing tablet

■ a pen or pencil

■ the Writing Worksheet you started at the end of Lesson 1

By the time you've finished Steps 1, 2 and 3 of your writing plan, you've gone a long way towards making sure your writing communicates clearly and effectively.

You have a pretty good idea about how readers are likely to respond to your message. You know whether your primary purpose is to influence readers or to inform them. And you have already put your most important message — what you want readers to do or to know — in words.

The steps you'll learn in this lesson take you through the process of **selecting the right information** to influence or inform readers and **organizing that information** so readers can follow your points easily.

When you finish the writing plan, you will have a logical, effective structure for the specific piece you are writing. Moving from plan to first draft will be easy. You won't have to think about how to get started, or what you want to say, or how you should organize your facts and ideas. You will have done that already.

**Before examining Steps 4, 5 and 6 of the planning process,
turn the page for an example of the entire process
from beginning to end.**

SITUATION: The writer, Sue, knows someone who would be perfect for the position of administrator in her friend Pete Starkey's company. Sue knows Pete has been swamped with applications, and she really wants him to consider her colleague.

Here are the steps you learned in Lesson 1:

1. Sue looks at what she's going to write from her **reader's** point of view:

   Pete is not expecting to hear from Sue; considers her knowledgeable; needs the information; is very busy; is anxious to fill the position; wants to interview only three candidates.

2. Sue knows that her primary purpose is to **influence** Pete.

3. Sue composes a **key sentence** that expresses what she wants Pete **to do**:

   "Hire Gail Schacter to fill the new administrative position in your company."

HERE ARE THE STEPS YOU WILL LEARN IN THIS LESSON:

4. Sue lists the **facts and ideas to accomplish her purpose** — all the reasons she can think of to answer Pete's obvious question, "**Why** should I hire Gail Schacter?"

- leader
- strong team member
- self-starter
- friendly
- good sense of humor
- communicates clearly
- finishes what she starts
- gives credit where due
- represents company well
- high management potential
- attentive to detail
- reports are accurate
- tactful
- encourages others to do their best
- conscientious
- sensitive
- does not need to be told what to do
- revised procedures manuals on her own
- never loses sight of "big picture"

5. Sue **groups the points** on her list into categories and decides what information belongs in what category. She comes up with five categories, or "**key points**":

high management potential	self-starter
conscientious	represents company well
strong team member	

6. Sue writes a **summary sentence** for each key point and puts the sentences in the order she thinks will be most effective. Under each sentence, she lists the points she plans to include in that category.

Pete should hire Sue's friend because:

She has high management potential
— leader
— communicates clearly
— never loses sight of "big picture"

She is a self-starter
— does not need to be told what to do
— revised procedures manual on her own

She is conscientious
— attentive to detail
— reports are accurate
— finishes what she starts

She is a strong team member
— gives credit where due
— encourages others to do their best

She represents the company well
— tactful
— friendly
— sensitive
— good sense of humor

Turn the page for a look at the letter Sue wrote.

Notice that Sue only had to add an opening, a few transitions, and a closing to transform her writing plan into a finished letter.

Dear Pete:

I heard that you're trying to fill the new administrative position in your department. Look no further--I have the perfect person for the job. **I strongly recommend that you hire my colleague, Gail Schacter.**

I have always felt that **Gail has high management potential.** A strong leader who communicates clearly, she never loses sight of the "big picture." Those are qualities the person you hire needs to have.

Gail has shown herself to be a true self-starter who needs little direction. She finds out what needs doing and gets it done. We were very pleased by the way she took it upon herself to revise our outdated procedures manual; the manual now serves as a model for other departments.

You'll quickly discover that Gail is very conscientious. She is attentive to detail and her reports are always accurate because she takes the time to check her facts carefully. I have noticed that once she starts a project, she stays with it until it is completed to her satisfaction.

Another of Gail's attributes should be of particular interest to you: **She's a very strong team member.** Time after time I have seen her encourage others to do their best, and she is always quick to give credit where credit is due.

Finally, because the position requires working with the public, you'll want to know that **Gail represents the company well.** Tactful, friendly, and sensitive to others, she also has a great sense of humor--and knows when to use it.

I've enclosed Gail's resume and urge you to give her your serious consideration. She'd be a valuable addition to your staff.

At the end of this lesson, you'll practice these steps by developing a writing plan for a situation of your own.

STEP 4 LIST THE FACTS AND IDEAS THAT WILL
ACCOMPLISH YOUR PURPOSE.

When you start to write something, you usually have a general idea
about what information to include. But you still have to determine
exactly what facts and ideas readers need to be convinced or
informed.

Start by writing down every fact or idea that might influence or inform
readers.

This process is called **brainstorming.** It may be familiar to you from
other contexts — for example, people use brainstorming techniques
to come up with creative solutions for problems.

The key is giving yourself permission to write down **every** point that
comes to mind when you ask:

WRITING TO **WHY** should readers do what I want them to do?
INFLUENCE

WRITING TO **WHAT** do readers need to know?
INFORM

At this stage of the planning process, it's very important to **write
quickly** without blocking the flow of ideas by evaluating items on your
list. In Step 5, you'll decide which items to keep and which to throw
out.

Try this process yourself with a simple practice situation. (If you
prefer, use a situation of your own. For this first practice, make sure
your purpose is to **influence** someone to do something.)

PRACTICE SITUATION: It's important that someone stay in your
house or apartment while you're away on vacation. Think of a friend or
colleague who might be willing to housesit for three weeks. Write the
person's name here:

_____

_____

**Now, turn the page and complete the three steps
in the writing process you learned in Lesson 1.**

STEPS 1–3   1. Look at what you're going to write from your **reader's** point of view:

IS THE READER . . .

☐ expecting to hear from you?

☐ familiar with the subject?

☐ already interested in what you have to say?

☐ likely to consider you an authority on the subject?

☐ likely to find what you have to say useful?

☐ familiar with your views on the subject?

☐ already committed to a point of view?

☐ likely to agree with your point of view?

☐ likely to find your message uncomfortable?

2. In this situation, you want to **influence** your reader.

3. Compose a **key sentence** that expresses your most important point — in this situation, what you want your reader **to do.**

EXAMPLE: "I want Anne Walker to housesit for me from March 1–20 while I am on vacation in Hawaii."

YOUR SENTENCE: I want _____ to _____

_____

_____

Now you're ready to come up with the information that will **influence** your reader.

4. List the **facts and ideas** that will accomplish your purpose — In this case, all the reasons you can think of to answer the reader's question, "**Why** should I housesit for you?"

_____ _____

_____ _____

_____ _____

_____ _____

_____ _____

Now **read through your list quickly.** Look at each item from your **reader's** point of view.

Cross out any items that do not directly answer the reader's question, "Why should I housesit for you?"

EXAMPLE: Suppose you wrote the following points. Only the points in italics directly address the reader's concerns. The others might be important to you, but they may not be of direct interest to your reader.

[My reader] should housesit while I'm on vacation because:

■ *Her children will enjoy using my pool.*

■ I need someone to water my plants.

■ *My house is 15 minutes closer to her job.*

■ I'll have a better time knowing someone is watching the house.

■ *I know she likes to entertain — I have a great kitchen.*

**Turn the page for more practice
deciding what information to include
when you write.**

PRACTICE

Read the situation. Then follow the instructions to complete Steps 1–4 of the planning process.

SITUATION: You are applying for a specific job, either within or outside of your organization. You are planning a letter or memo that will encourage the person who does the hiring to consider you for the job.

NOTE   Be sure to choose a real job that you would like to have.

STEPS 1–3

1. Look at what you're going to write from your **reader's** point of view:

   READER'S NAME OR DESCRIPTION: _____

   _____

   IS READER . . .

   ☐ expecting to hear from you?

   ☐ familiar with the subject?

   ☐ already interested in what you have to say?

   ☐ likely to consider you an authority on the subject?

   ☐ likely to find what you have to say useful?

   ☐ familiar with your views on the subject?

   ☐ already committed to a point of view?

   ☐ likely to agree with your point of view?

   ☐ likely to find your message uncomfortable?

2. Decide what you want to accomplish:

   ☑ **INFLUENCE** the reader   ☐ **INFORM** the reader
   to hire you   about your qualifications

   In this situation, there is definitely something you want your reader to do — hire you. So it's more effective if your primary purpose is to **influence** your reader.

3. Compose a **key sentence** that says exactly what you want the reader to do:

   I want my reader to _____

   _____

❖ **HINT**   Your key sentence should clearly state what you want your reader to do: "**Hire** me for the computer sales job"; "**Consider** me for the position of marketing department manager"; etc.

On the next page, you will complete Step 4 by listing the facts and ideas that will accomplish your purpose.

STEP 4   LIST THE FACTS AND IDEAS THAT WILL
ACCOMPLISH YOUR PURPOSE

Now you're ready to come up with the information that will influence your reader to consider you for the job. Remember to keep your **reader's point of view** in mind and look for points that will be of direct interest to that person.

List the **facts and ideas that will accomplish your purpose** — all the reasons you can think of to answer the reader's question, "Why should

I consider _____ for this job?"

your name

Use as many lines as you need.

Consider me for this job because:

_____	_____
_____	_____
_____	_____
_____	_____
_____	_____
_____	_____
_____	_____
_____	_____
_____	_____
_____	_____
_____	

Now read through the list quickly. Cross out any points that are important from your point of view but would not help convince the reader to consider you for the job.

EXAMPLE   The fact that you need more money is of great interest to you, but it is probably not going to carry a lot of weight in your reader's mind.

To determine whether you're the right person for a job, the reader needs to know about your experience, reliability, skills, etc. The fact that you have five years' experience would be far more convincing than, "I want a shorter commute."

**Now that you know how to determine what facts and ideas
to include in your writing, turn the page for Step 5,
where you'll learn how to organize the
information logically and effectively.**

STEP 5   GROUP POINTS INTO CATEGORIES

Whenever you write anything longer than a few sentences, it is important to organize — or group — your facts and ideas into categories. These categories provide the reader with a road map, a route through the information.

Grouping is a way of organizing information to help people understand it. For example, look at how people learn long-distance phone numbers. Try learning this number:

5135553938

Hard, isn't it? But the number is much easier to learn if it's broken down into groups:

AREA CODE	PREFIX	NUMBER
(513)	555	3938

In the same way, writers can help readers understand what they have to say by grouping information into related topics.

Grouping points during the planning process also makes writing easier because you don't have to worry about where to begin paragraphs. As you'll see, each group, or topic, usually forms one paragraph.

There is no standard way to organize information. It is a highly individual process that emerges from the situation and your own unique perceptions of what things have in common.

Try it. What do the items in each of these groups have in common?

Group A	Group B
wrenches	staplers
hammers	scissors
paint	white-out

It's easy to see that the items in Group A are construction supplies, while those in Group B are office supplies.

You could also group the items this way:

Group A	Group B
paint	wrenches
white-out	hammers
	staplers
	scissors

Now the items in Group A are disposable and the ones in Group B are non-disposable.

The grouping of facts and ideas is your **organizational scheme.** The scheme you use depends mostly on the type of information and what you want to accomplish by writing.

The organizational scheme is more useful than a conventional outline because it lets the information determine the organization. In a conventional outline, you tend to start with the categories before you know what information you'll include. It's like forcing your family to fit a house that already exists, rather than letting the size and needs of your family determine the size and layout of the house you build.

Here are some typical organizational schemes:

TOPICS   Suppose you are providing readers with details about three computer systems. You might group information into these categories:

> COST
> SIZE
> SPECIAL FEATURES

CHRONO-LOGICAL ORDER   Use this way of grouping information when you want to show events or actions over time. For instance, you might use either of these organizational schemes to present information about a long-term research project:

SCHEME 1	**SCHEME 2**
FIRST YEAR	PAST HISTORY
SECOND YEAR	PRESENT STATUS
THIRD YEAR	PROJECTION FOR FUTURE

COMPARISON AND CONTRAST   Sometimes it's most effective to organize information into two categories and compare them. You might use one of these schemes to give managers details for evaluating whether a particular building is suitable for your company's new offices:

SCHEME 1:   PROS/CONS

SCHEME 2:   ADVANTAGES/DISADVANTAGES

SCHEME 3:   MEETS/FAILS TO MEET OUR CRITERIA

PRACTICE

Here's a list of food items. Imagine you're writing a report or magazine article on food. Organize the food items into two or three logical groups.

chocolate ice cream   sweet and sour pork
spaghetti   strawberries
hamburgers   artichokes
spare ribs   pecan pie
cheese Danish   roast turkey
crab   walnut torte

ANSWERS TO PRACTICE

Here are some ways of grouping the foods on the list. You may have grouped them differently. It's only important that you found some logical organizational scheme.

TOPICS

Main Courses	Fruits & Veggies	Desserts
sweet & sour pork	artichokes	chocolate ice cream
spaghetti	strawberries	cheese Danish
roast turkey		pecan pie
hamburgers		walnut torte
spare ribs		
crab		

TOPICS

High in Vitamins	High in Protein	High in Starch
strawberries	chocolate ice cream	spaghetti
artichokes	hamburgers	cheese Danish
	spare ribs	pecan pie
	crab	walnut torte
	sweet and sour pork	
	roast turkey	

COMPARISON & CONTRAST — PROS & CONS

Foods I Like	Foods I Dislike
chocolate ice cream	hamburgers
cheese Danish	pecan pie
roast turkey	artichokes
spare ribs	spaghetti
sweet & sour pork	walnut torte
strawberries	
crab	

**There's another practice
on the next page.**

PRACTICE

Suppose you are writing a magazine article about these athletic activities:

Surfing	Basketball
Skiing	Canoeing
Wind Surfing	Tennis
Snowboarding	Volleyball
Mountain Biking	Baseball
Rollerblading	Mountain Climbing
Swimming	Rock Climbing
Scuba Diving	Kayaking
Football	Jogging

Here's one way to organize the activities:

WATERSPORTS	**NON-WATER SPORTS**
Surfing	Basketball
Canoeing	Skiing
Wind Surfing	Tennis
Swimming	Volleyball
Scuba Diving	Baseball
Kayaking	Mountain Climbing
	Snowboarding
	Mountain Biking
	Rollerblading
	Rock Climbing
	Football
	Jogging

Now you try it. Organize the activities another way:

ANSWER TO PRACTICE

Here is one way you might have grouped the activities:

COSTLY

Canoeing
Skiing
Scuba Diving
Mountain Biking
Wind Surfing
Snowboarding
Kayaking

LITTLE OR NO COST

Swimming
Football
Basketball
Volleyball
Baseball
Jogging

MODERATELY EXPENSIVE

Surfing
Tennis
Mountain Climbing
Rock Climbing
Rollerblading

STEP 6   WRITE A SUMMARY SENTENCE FOR EACH CATEGORY
               AND LIST THE SENTENCES IN ORDER

Earlier you learned that each category of information will usually form a paragraph when you write your draft.

The **summary sentence** expands the category into a statement introducing the points in the paragraph and telling readers why they are important. Without the context the summary sentence provides, readers might have trouble following your points or miss important points altogether.

You might experience a similar kind of frustration during certain telephone conversations. Imagine you are very busy trying to meet a deadline. You receive this call from a colleague you know only slightly.

YOU	"Hello?"
CALLER	"Hi! This is Jane Smith. I have bad news."
YOU	"I'm sorry — what's wrong?"
CALLER	"My car is in the shop for repairs."
YOU	"Oh? That's a shame."
CALLER	"It won't be ready until Thursday or Friday."
YOU	"Well, that's the way those things go, isn't it?"
CALLER	"And they refused to give me a loaner."
YOU	(Confused — and ready to get back to work) "Hm....Jane, why are you telling me all this?"
CALLER	"Oh — don't you see? **I won't be able to meet you for lunch on Wednesday...."**
YOU	"... because your car is in the shop for repairs, right?"
CALLER	"Right!"

Jane's message would have been much clearer and would have taken much less time if she had said right away that **she could not meet you for lunch on Wednesday** because her car was in the shop. The information about the car is meaningful to you only when it is clearly related to the lunch meeting.

To write a **summary sentence**, simply expand the category heading into a statement that directly answers the reader's question: "Why should I do what you want me to do?"

SITUATION: Jason wants to influence his manager, Sarah, to **authorize the purchase of a desktop publishing system** for his department.

Jason knows Sarah's question will be, "Why should I authorize this purchase?" To answer the question, he came up with these points:

■ increased workload	■ increasing production delays
■ more departments using production facilities	■ missing deadlines
■ will save company $$ in long run	■ will be developing user manuals & quarterly reports
■ less need to hire extra staff	■ writers & editors can do layout, some graphics

Here's how Jason grouped these points:

CATEGORY **Production delays**
■ more departments using production facilities — delays of 5 days or more
■ missed several deadlines this year — materials late

CATEGORY **Increased workload**
■ will be developing user manuals & quarterly reports

CATEGORY **Save $$**
■ writers, editors can do layout, some graphics themselves
■ less need for us to hire extra staff

To complete his writing plan, Jason developed a summary sentence for each category by adding a few words to the category heading:

WRITING PLAN

Sarah should authorize the purchase of a desktop publishing system for my department because:

Production Delays

We are experiencing too many production delays

■ more departments using production facilities — delays of 5 days or more

■ missed several deadlines this year — materials late

Increased Workload

Our workload continues to increase

■ will be developing user manuals & quarterly reports

Save $$

A system of our own will more than pay for itself

■ writers, editors can do layout, some graphics themselves

■ less need for us to hire extra staff

Turn the page to see the finished memo.

Here's how the writing plan provides the logical structure for the memo. Notice how the **summary sentences** start each paragraph.

TO: Sarah
FROM: Jason
RE: Desktop Publishing System

Sarah,

As we discussed last week, I think it's very important for you to **authorize the purchase of a desktop publishing system** for my department.

Since the re-organization, **we have been experiencing far too many production delays.** In fact, so many departments are using the production facilities that delays of five days or more have become routine. We've been unable to meet several deadlines this year because our materials weren't ready on time.

This problem continues to get worse because **our workload continues to increase.** We're now responsible for developing user manuals for the new product line. In addition, we've been asked to write all the quarterly reports.

My calculations show that **a system of our own will more than pay for itself** within six months. The writers and editors will be able to do the layout and some of the graphics themselves, reducing the need for us to hire extra people during peak periods. The enclosed materials include a chart showing projected savings over the next two years.

Please let me know if you need more information. Otherwise, I'll stop by on Friday to see what decision you've made.

Thanks,

Jason

**Turn to the next page for some practice writing
summary sentences for another situation.**

PRACTICE

SITUATION: Your employees' group wants to convince your CEO to provide an in-house exercise facility. As the group's representative, you have been asked to draft a memo asking the CEO to allocate funds for the facility.

Steps 1–5 of the writing plan have been completed for you. Read them, then complete Step 6.

1. Look at what you're going to write from your **reader's** point of view.

   ■ The CEO is not expecting to hear from me.

   ■ She is familiar with the employees' need for this facility.

   ■ She may be reluctant to spend money.

2. Decide what you want to accomplish.

   In this situation, you definitely want to **influence** your reader.

3. Compose a **key sentence** that expresses your most important message.

   "Please allocate funds for an in-house exercise facility for employees."

4. List the **facts and ideas** that will accomplish your purpose.

   The CEO should allocate funds for an exercise facility because:

   - saves money — less absenteeism because people who exercise are less likely to get sick

   - shows company cares about employees

   - better team spirit when people work out together

   - reduces cost of health insurance — healthy people have fewer claims

   - gives people something to look forward to — happier

   - would be one of first companies in area to invest in exercise facility

5. **Group** points into categories

   MORALE

   - better team spirit when people work out together

   - gives people something to look forward to — happier

   FINANCIAL

   - saves money — less absenteeism because people who exercise are less likely to get sick

   - reduces cost of health insurance — healthy people have fewer claims

   REPUTATION

   - shows company cares about employees

   - would be one of first companies in area to invest in exercise facility

---

Now follow the instructions on the next page to complete Step 6, writing summary sentences.

STEP 6   WRITE A SUMMARY SENTENCE FOR EACH
CATEGORY AND LIST SENTENCES IN ORDER

To complete Step 6, you will write a **summary sentence** for each of the three categories developed in Step 5: "Morale," "Financial," and "Reputation."

Remember, when you are writing to **influence** — as in this situation — the **summary sentence** directly answers the question "Why should my reader do what I want him or her to do?"

Here are the categories from Step 5. For each category, **write one complete sentence** that directly answers the question, "Why should the CEO allocate funds for an exercise facility?"

MORALE

■ better team spirit when people work out together

■ gives people something to look forward to — happier

SUMMARY SENTENCE _____

_____

_____

_____

FINANCIAL

■ saves money — less absenteeism because people who exercise are less likely to get sick

■ reduces cost of health insurance — healthy people have fewer claims

SUMMARY SENTENCE _____

_____

_____

_____

REPUTATION

■ shows company cares about employees

■ would be one of the first companies in area to invest in exercise facility

SUMMARY SENTENCE _____

_____

_____

_____

Check your answers on the next page.

Here are examples of the kinds of summary sentences you may have written.

Your sentences are probably a little different, and they may be very different. That's fine.

The important point is that each sentence should directly answer the question, **"Why should the CEO allocate funds for an exercise facility?"**

MORALE

EXAMPLE   An exercise facility will improve employees' morale.

EXAMPLE   Exercise is good for morale.

FINANCIAL

EXAMPLE   The company would save money by installing an exercise facility.

EXAMPLE   Exercise facilities can save the company money.

REPUTATION

EXAMPLE   Building an exercise facility would do wonders for the company's reputation.

EXAMPLE   Exercise facilities will help give us a positive image.

There's only one thing left to do.

You now have a complete writing plan for the memo to the CEO. The only thing you still need to do is decide on the **best order** for the summary sentences.

When determining what information goes first, second, and so on, consider this: Put the summary sentence that your reader is likely to consider the most important **first**.

When people read quickly, they tend to pick up beginnings and endings. By putting the most important point first, you increase your chances of catching and keeping the reader's attention.

You can then, if you wish, put your second most important point last, unless the information dictates some other order.

Look at the summary sentences below. Which point do you think is most likely to convince the CEO to allocate funds for an exercise facility? Number the sentences in the order you think would be best.

_____ **Exercise facilities will help give us a positive image.**

_____ **Exercise facilities can save the company money.**

_____ **An exercise facility will improve employees' morale.**

Here's the order one writer chose, based on the assumption that saving money was of most concern to her company's CEO:

1. Exercise facilities can save the company money.

2. Exercise facilities will help give us a positive image.

3. An exercise facility will improve employees' morale.

Completed Writing Plan

Here is an example of the writing plan. Notice the way it creates a "blueprint" for the memo.

READER: CEO

PURPOSE: To influence

KEY SENTENCE: Our employees' group would like you to allocate funds for an in-house exercise facility.

MAIN POINTS:

1. Exercise facilities can save the company money.

   ■ less absenteeism because people who exercise are less likely to get sick

   ■ reduced cost of health insurance — healthy people have fewer claims

2. Exercise facilities will help give us a positive image.

   ■ way to show that company cares about employees

   ■ would be one of the first companies in area to invest in such a facility

3. An exercise facility will improve employees' morale.

   ■ increase team spirit by working out together

   ■ give people something to look forward to — happier

Finished Memo

Notice that the most important message is right in the first paragraph and the structure of the memo comes directly from the writing plan.

TO: Anna Harbin
FROM: Acme Employees' Association
RE: Exercise Facility

Anna,

After some months of discussion about ways to improve our working environment, we've decided that **we'd like you to allocate funds for an in-house exercise facility.**

Our research on this topic makes it clear that **exercise facilities can save companies money.** For instance, people who exercise are less likely to get sick, which means that less money is lost to absenteeism. Also, healthy employees have fewer insurance claims, thus reducing health insurance costs.

An exercise facility will help give us the positive image we are constantly seeking by demonstrating that the company cares about its employees. We have a unique opportunity to become known as one of the first companies in the area to invest in such a facility.

We also believe that **an exercise facility will improve our employees' morale.** Working out together is a great way to increase team spirit. People also say they would be happier if they had an exercise session to look forward to at lunch or after work.

We've enclosed a summary of the facts we collected--we think you'll find them convincing. Please let us know if you need more information. Thanks for considering this request.

Writing to Inform

So far, we've looked at examples of the planning process when the purpose is **to influence.**

When you write primarily **to inform**, the process changes slightly. Instead of asking, "Why should readers do what I want them to do," ask, "**WHAT** do readers need to know?" It's your answers to that question that make up the list of facts and ideas to include.

Here's an example.

SITUATION   Joan Huang is in charge of the conference on "Newest Trends in Evaluating Performance." She wants everyone in her department to know what will be covered during the conference and how to make arrangements to attend.

READERS   Joan's staff

PURPOSE   To inform

KEY SENTENCE   Here is the current information on the upcoming conference, "Newest Trends in Evaluating Performance."

Joan asks, "**What** does my staff need to know," and lists these questions:

- What will be covered at the conference?
- Who will be speaking
- Where will it be held?
- Dates and times?
- What if I can't attend?
- How and where do I sign up?
- Who is responsible for travel and housing arrangements?
- Who's paying the air fare and hotel expenses?

Next, Joan **answers** the questions:

■ What will be covered at the conference?
   – Newest computer-based appraisal systems being tested in the U.S., Great Britain, Japan
   – Case studies: 360° feedback
   – Peer evaluations — training methods

■ Who will be speaking?
   – Representatives from National Institute of Performance
   – Representatives of the National Human Resources Organization
   – Executives from leading European organizations
   – Faculty members from the University of California Business School

■ Where will it be held?
   – Marriott Hotel, San Francisco
   – Crown Room

■ Dates and times?
   – February 14, 15
   – 9 a.m. – 5 p.m. each day
   – Complete agenda available week before conference

■ What if I can't attend?
   – Ask Josie in Office for presentation reports

■ How and where do I sign up?
   – Josie has all the forms — due January 31

■ Who is responsible for travel and housing arrangements?
   – Sue at Whole Universe Travel

■ Who's paying the air fare and hotel expenses?
   – The company

Joan groups the points into **categories**. Then she writes a **summary sentence** for each category and puts them in order.

- ■ **Logistics**: The conference is scheduled for February 14 and 15.

- ■ **Topics**: Representatives from various organizations will make presentations on the newest performance evaluation strategies.

- ■ **Speakers**: Speakers include experts in the field from business and academic organizations in the United States and abroad.

- ■ **Arrangements**: The company is paying all expenses. Here's how to make arrangements and receive presentation reports if you cannot attend.

Completed Memo

To: Department Members

From: Joan Huang, Department Manager

Subject: Annual Conference

Here is the information you've been waiting for about the upcoming conference on "Newest Trends in Evaluating Performance."

Logistics

The conference is scheduled for February 14 and 15. All events will take place in the Crown Room of the San Francisco Marriott Hotel between 9:00 a.m. and 5:00 p.m. A detailed agenda will be available the week of February 6.

Topics

Representatives from various organizations will make presentations on the newest performance evaluation strategies, including:

- • The newest computer-based appraisal systems now being tested in the United States, Great Britain, and Japan

- • Case studies that explore the advantages and pitfalls of using 360° feedback

- • Methods of preparing employees to conduct successful peer evaluations

Speakers

Speakers include experts in the field from business organizations and academic institutions in the United States and abroad. We expect representatives from the National Institute of Performance, the National Human Resources Organization, leading European organizations, and the University of California Business School.

Arrangements

The company is paying all expenses. Here's how to make arrangements or receive the presentation reports if you cannot attend:

- To sign up: Call Josie at extension 405 for a registration form. Make sure to return the form to Josie by 5:00 p.m. on January 31.

- To make air and hotel reservations: Call Sue at Whole Universe Travel, 361-9275.

- If you cannot attend: Ask Josie to put your name on the distribution list for presentation reports.

If you have any questions about this conference, call me at extension 263. I hope you are able to attend.

Now turn the page for some guidelines for sending Email messages

Sending Email Messages

Email came along so fast that people are making up the rules on the spot. Although some "conventions" have been established, there is still little consistency in terms of style or format.

What's important to keep in mind is that Email is simply a form of **writing**. Effective Email communications require the same thought and planning as any other written documents. They also require attention to some considerations that are specific to this medium.

Here's an example of an Email message that's hard to follow:

```
TO:       Sue Gabel
SUBJECT:  Update

Hi Sue here are the ecr leader guide files, better
late than never!! Thanks for your message. will let
you know where I want the FedEx package to go,
Robert and I are in today so wecan get some CRC to
production and go to the anual meeting. After that
we may either be at my or laura's house,--not sure
yet but Ill keep you posted one way or another.
```

And one that's easy to understand.

```
TO:       Sue Gabel
SUBJECT:  Update on current projects

Sue - Here are a few notes on our current projects:

• Attached are the leaders' guides for the
  Economic Community Refinancing course. Sorry
  they're late.

• I'll let you know where to send the FedEx
  package as soon as I find the address.

• Robert and I are in the office today. We plan on
  sending at least 3 sections of the Credit
  Reporting course to production and still have
  time to get to the annual meeting.

• After today, we will work at Laura's house or
  mine for the rest of the week. We'll keep you
  posted.
```

Here are guidelines for making sure that your Email messages are clear and present a positive image of you and your organization.

■ **Plan what you write.** Composing an Email might feel more like having a conversation than writing a memo, but it is still writing. To avoid rambling, think about your reader, your purpose, your main point, and what details to include. You may not need to complete a Writing Worksheet for a brief message, but it's always helpful to jot down the points you plan to include.

■ **Pay attention to your audience.** Review your distribution list regularly and send Emails only to people who need the information. And think carefully before forwarding an Email message.

■ **Make sure Email is the appropriate choice for the message.** Some information is too sensitive to be sent through such a public medium. For example, never use Email to criticize or convey confidential information; you might as well shout down the hall.

■ **Consider the tone.** The casual quality of Email can result in a tone that is more brusque or abrupt than you intended.

■ **Keep Email messages short.** Try to limit the message to what the recipient can read on one screen. Send longer documents as attachments.

■ **Keep sentences and paragraphs short.** It's harder to read from a screen than from paper. Limit sentences to 18–22 words and paragraphs to 3–5 lines. One-sentence paragraphs are fine.

■ **Use lists whenever you can.** They're easy to write and easy to read. (See Lesson 3 for more on using lists.)

■ **Pay attention to the formatting.** Messages with all caps or all lower case letters, no breaks between paragraphs or list items, and uneven spacing are hard to read and they look even worse printed out.

■ **Follow the rules of grammar, punctuation, spelling and word usage**. Not only do they help readers understand your message, but sloppy writing indicates sloppy thinking, even on a computer screen.

■ **Avoid fancy graphics and visuals.** Graphics don't always come through the way you intended them, and visuals can take a long time to load.

■ **Tell people how to reach you.** Include a signature line with your full name, company (and/or department), and phone number. Consider including your fax number and mailing address.

■ **Delete unnecessary information.** When replying to or forwarding an Email, delete any information the recipient does not need. For example, delete previous messages unless the recipient needs them to understand your message.

■ **Write useful subject lines.** Tell readers what the message is about. For example, instead of writing, "Thrombos," write, "Need thrombos by Thursday." If you are sending information that requires no response, include FYI in the subject line: "FYI: Decisions made at 9/6 meeting."

■ **Use pronouns carefully.** Pronouns such as "this," "it," "he," and "she" will confuse readers unless they clearly refer to specific nouns. If there's any doubt, use the nouns instead.

■ **Include enough information to provide a context for your message.** For example, if you are responding to a recipient's questions, restate, summarize, or list the questions, or include a copy of the person's original message (condensed, if possible).

Review

You've reached the end of Lesson 2. Before applying what you've learned to a writing situation of your own, answer these review questions.

Write the correct word in the blanks. If you're not sure what to write or want to check your answer, turn to the page in parentheses to the right of the sentence.

1. To decide what information to include when you

    write, list the _____ and

    _____ that will accomplish your

    purpose.   (45)

2. If you're writing to influence readers, ask

    "_____ should readers do what I want them to do?"   (45)

3. If you're writing to inform readers, ask

    "_____ do readers need to know?"

4. After listing the facts and ideas to include in your writing,

    the next step is to _____ points into categories.   (52)

5. A _____ _____ expands the
    category headings into a statement that introduces
    points and tells readers why they are important.   (61)

ASSIGNMENT

Now you know how the planning process works. Before starting the next lesson, try the entire process with a writing situation of your own.

You have two options:

1. Complete Steps 4, 5 and 6 on the Writing Worksheet you started at the end of Lesson 1.

—OR—

2. Remove a new Worksheet from the back of this book and complete Steps 1–6 for a new writing situation.

When you have finished the writing plan, you may:

■ Set it aside and move on to Lesson 3, where you'll learn to use the plan to write a first draft.

—OR—

■ Do a quick first draft before beginning Lesson 3 and choose another situation for the assignment at the end of Lesson 3.

What's Next?

In Lesson 3 you will learn to use your writing plan to write a first draft. You'll see that you've already done most of the work. Only the final shaping is left.

LESSON 3.
WRITING THE FIRST DRAFT

L E S S O N   3
Writing the First Draft

Introduction

When you have a completed writing plan, the first draft almost writes itself. You've already done the hard work — deciding what you want to accomplish, finding the right words to express your main point, and selecting and organizing the facts and ideas you need to influence or inform readers.

The next step is to use that plan to write a first draft.

OBJECTIVES   In this lesson, you'll learn to write a first draft by:

■ Reviewing your writing plan and revising it as needed to make sure it is sound

■ Writing an opening that catches readers' attention and clearly says what you are writing about

■ Using transitions to link points, paragraphs, and sections smoothly

■ Using lists to present information so readers can grasp it quickly

■ Writing a closing that sums up points as needed and tells readers clearly what happens next

WHAT YOU NEED

■ a writing tablet

■ a pen or pencil

■ any Writing Worksheets you completed in Lessons 1 and 2

Reviewing Your Writing Plan

Before starting the first draft, take a few moments to review your writing plan. There are two reasons for doing this:

■ If there are any inconsistencies in the plan, it's important to correct them before you begin the first draft

■ Reading the plan through helps you keep it in mind when you start writing, particularly if time has passed since you finished the plan

Here are some questions to ask as you review your writing plan:

■ Have I considered my **reader's** point of view?

■ Have I correctly identified my **primary purpose**?

■ Does my **key sentence** express exactly what I want my reader to do or to know?

■ Does each **summary sentence** . . . .

Writing to influence	explain why readers should do what I want them to do?
Writing to inform	introduce and/or summarize what readers need to know?

■ Have I eliminated **unnecessary** information?

■ Have I included all **necessary** information?

■ Have I **organized the information** logically and effectively — from the reader's point of view?

If you answer "no" to any of these questions, take a closer look at your writing plan. **Before** you start the first draft, be sure the plan accurately expresses what you intend to say.

Writing the Opening

The first few lines of any piece of writing are extremely important. It is in the opening paragraph that you must catch your reader's attention, set the right tone, and make it clear what you are writing about.

Read these two openings. Which opening makes you want to continue?

MEMO 1   This is in reference to your recent letter
         which was passed to this department for
         review. Unfortunately, the information you
         requested is not available at this point
         in time . . .

MEMO 2   Thanks for asking about the August 5th
         Computer Class. I'm sorry that we do not
         yet know the instructor's name or the
         location, but we should be able to send
         you all the details by July 15.

You probably preferred the opening of Memo 2. The first opening uses a lot of cliches such as, "This is in reference to . . . ." It communicates little specific information.

The opening of the second memo, however, was clearly written by one person to another. It responds directly to specific questions. The writer gets to the point quickly and provides details.

Here are the criteria for an effective opening:

■ It makes a personal contact with the reader and sets the right tone — particularly important when your primary purpose is to influence

■ It catches the reader's attention

■ It includes a key sentence that tells the reader what you are writing about

■ It is no more than three or four sentences long

Here are some examples of openings. In each set, put an "X" next to the opening you think best meets the criteria.

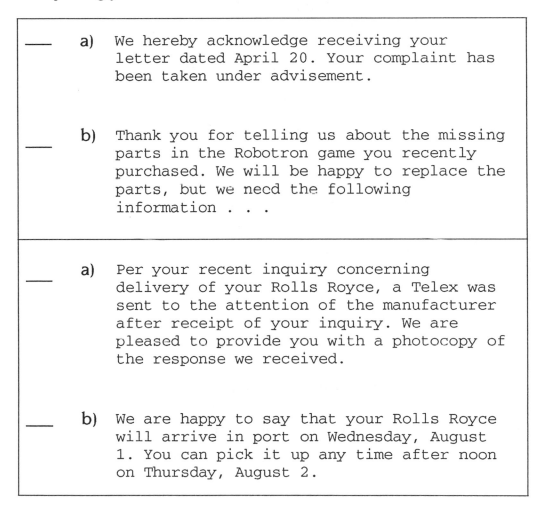

_____ **a)** We hereby acknowledge receiving your letter dated April 20. Your complaint has been taken under advisement.

_____ **b)** Thank you for telling us about the missing parts in the Robotron game you recently purchased. We will be happy to replace the parts, but we need the following information . . .

_____ **a)** Per your recent inquiry concerning delivery of your Rolls Royce, a Telex was sent to the attention of the manufacturer after receipt of your inquiry. We are pleased to provide you with a photocopy of the response we received.

_____ **b)** We are happy to say that your Rolls Royce will arrive in port on Wednesday, August 1. You can pick it up any time after noon on Thursday, August 2.

If you preferred version "b" in both sets, you recognize an effective opening.

One quick way to improve openings is to avoid overused phrases such as:

With reference to . . .

Pursuant to . . .

Enclosed please find . . .

Please be advised . . .

Attached herewith . . .

I am writing to inform you . . .

Regarding your recent communication . . .

We are in receipt of your letter . . .

On the above date and time . . .

This is in regards to . . .

Per your request . . .

Here are some examples of how to replace overused phrases with simple, direct language:

Per your request for shipping instructions . . .

As you asked, here are the instructions for preparing your shipment.

Please be advised that your shipment has been delayed.

Unfortunately, your shipment has been delayed.

Enclosed please find copies of your last three invoices.

I have enclosed copies of your last three invoices.

I am sending copies of your last three invoices.

Here are copies of your last three invoices.

I am writing to inform you that your shipment has been located.

We have found your shipment.

This is in regards to your recent communication regarding the replacement parts.

We are sorry that the replacement parts we sent do not fit your model.

We are in receipt of your 12/05/99 letter in regards to the vacant position.

As you asked in your recent letter, we will be happy to send you an application for the position of Community Relations Director.

On the above date and time a signature was obtained for the delivery of the payment.

Our records show that Ms. Ellen McDonald signed for the check on January 5, 2000, at 1500 hours.

On the next page, practice rewriting weak openings.

PRACTICE

Using your imagination to fill in missing details, revise the following openings so they:

■ make a personal contact with the reader, set the right tone, and catch the reader's attention

■ include a key sentence that tells the reader what you are writing about

■ are no more than three or four sentences long

❖ HINT

It will be easier to revise the openings if you look at the message from the **reader's** point of view.

OPENING 1

```
Please be advised that your comments on the
proposed Computer Training Program, received by
this office on June 3, have been reviewed and,
where appropriate, incorporated into the Program.
```

_____

_____

_____

_____

_____

_____

OPENING 2

I am writing to inform you that payment has not yet been received for the current month. The conditions of your Note specify that payment be made no later than the first day of each month. It is imperative that payment be received within 10 days of the date of this letter.

_____

_____

_____

_____

_____

_____

OPENING 3

Attached please find a copy of the Assistant Director's letter to Acme Products. Also attached is a copy of the letter to Alex Stein from Acme's CEO, as well as a copy of the Test Plan which was written by Bill Jordan.

_____

_____

_____

_____

_____

_____

**Compare your revisions to the ones
on the next page.**

ANSWERS TO PRACTICE

Here are the kinds of changes you might have made.

OPENING 1

Original	Please be advised that your comments on the proposed Computer Training Program, received by this office on June 3, have been reviewed and, where appropriate, incorporated into the Program.
Revision	Thank you for your comments on the proposed Computer Training Program. We have incorporated the suggested changes listed below.

OPENING 2

Original	I am writing to inform you that payment has not yet been received for the current month. The conditions of your Note specify that payment be made no later than the first day of each month. It is imperative that payment be received within 10 days of the date of this letter.
Revision	We have not yet received the loan payment that was due on April 1. Please make sure we receive it no later than April 25.

OPENING 3

Original	Attached please find a copy of the Assistant Director's letter to Acme Products. Also attached is a copy of the letter to Alex Stein from Acme's CEO, as well as a copy of the Test Plan which was written by Bill Jordan.
Revision	I'm enclosing copies of the following: • the Assistant Director's letter to Acme Products • Acme's CEO's letter to Alex Stein • Bill Jordan's Test Plan

Now that you know how to write more
effective openings, turn the page
for a discussion of transitions.

Transitions

To make your writing more readable, use **transitions** to connect your ideas. A transition is a word, phrase or sentence that relates a new topic to the previous one, smoothly connecting the parts of a piece of writing.

Transitions are rather like the cartilage that holds your bones together. They form a link, a connective tissue. In writing, transitions show readers how your ideas fit together, help you achieve continuity, and help readers follow your points easily.

Read this memo. The highlighted words and phrases serve as **transitions**, helping the reader see the connection between points.

Alex--

Thanks for calling yesterday to ask about this year's sales conference. **As you know**, the Planning Committee is running a little behind schedule. **Nevertheless**, I'm happy to tell you what we know so far.

Despite the problem we had with meeting space last year, we've decided to give Lazy Acres another try. Everyone rates the other facilities very highly. **In particular**, people like the tennis courts and exercise equipment. **Also**, the guest rooms are spacious, so we can use them for small group meetings.

Although the date is still under discussion, we're looking at the second week in August. We are, **however, also** considering September; **for one thing**, the August date might interfere with people's vacation plans.

Unless we run into a snag, we hope to have firm plans by the end of the month. I'll let you know what I know as soon as I know it. **Until then**, feel free to pass this information on to your staff.

Here are examples of words and phrases you can use to link points, sections and paragraphs:

ADDITIONS

again	as well as	equally important
also	further	for one thing
and also	in addition	furthermore
as you asked	next	now
moreover	as you know	

CONTRASTS

despite	however	although
but	unless	until
nevertheless		

COMPARISONS

in the same way	similarly	equally

EMPHASIS

above all	certainly	especially
in fact	in other words	indeed
of course	in particular	

RESULT

accordingly	thus	as a result
consequently	for that reason	as a consequence

SUMMARY

finally	to sum up	on the whole

**See if you can identify transitions
in the letter on the next page.**

PRACTICE

Underline the transitions in this letter. Notice how they help link the points and improve the tone.

Dear Frieda:

As you asked, I am happy to suggest a marketing consultant for your new project. The person I recommend most highly is Kate Jackson.

I worked with Kate for two years at Vision West. Although we were in different departments, we worked together on at least five projects. She was reliable and pleasant. Best of all, she seemed to have a never-ending store of creative ideas, although she never tried to impose them on the group. In fact, she was quite willing to drop any plan that didn't seem workable.

Unless Kate's situation has changed since I last spoke to her in May, I suspect she will be very interested in your position. She will, of course, want to know something about the opportunities it offers for advancement.

I hope Kate works out for you. If not, give me a call and I'll keep my eyes open for someone else.

_____

**Turn the page for examples of transitions
you might have underlined.**

ANSWERS TO PRACTICE

Did you underline these transitions?

Dear Frieda:

    <u>As you asked</u>, I am happy to suggest a marketing consultant for your new project. The person I recommend most highly is Kate Jackson.

    I worked with Kate for two years at Vision West. <u>Although</u> we were in different departments, we worked together on at least five projects. She was reliable and pleasant. <u>Best of all</u>, she seemed to have a never-ending store of creative ideas, <u>although</u> she never tried to impose them on the group. <u>In fact</u>, she was quite willing to drop any plan that didn't seem workable.

    <u>Unless</u> Kate's situation has changed since I last spoke to her in May, I suspect she will be very interested in your position. She will, <u>of course</u>, want to know something about the opportunities it offers for advancement.

    I hope Kate works out for you. <u>If not</u>, give me a call and I'll keep my eyes open for someone else.

Using Lists

How do you read business documents? Chances are you don't linger over the words the way you'd linger over a novel. Instead, you scan the document to pick out the main points and the details you need.

Taking the reader's point of view, it's easy to see that paragraphs are seldom the best way to present information. The more technical or complicated the information, the more likely it is to be lost when presented in paragraph form.

Your goal as a writer is to help readers find information as quickly as possible. To do that, look for opportunities to present information in **lists**.

Read the examples on the next two pages. They both present the same information. But see how much easier the revision is to read.

ORIGINAL

Dear Ms. Fratelli:

To process your loan application, we need the following information and documents as soon as possible.

In Item 12A, please enter the name and address of the lender who holds your second deed of trust. The current balances on all your credit cards and outstanding loans should be entered in items 16B and 16C, except for your automobile loans (Item 16D).

The name and address of your previous employers should be entered in Item 6C if you have been at your current job for less than two years. Include an explanation of any gap in employment during the past ten years.

List the balances on your bank accounts in Item 4A. Include the name and address of the institution and the account number. Use items 4B, C, and D for Certificates of Deposit, stocks, etc., as shown.

The purpose of the loan should be entered in Item 3, along with the amount requested. Finally, be sure to sign and date the form in item 23. The completed form should be sent to the loan processor along with copies of your last two years' tax returns and copies of your most recent pay stubs.

Please let me know if you have questions.

Sincerely,

REVISION

Dear Ms. Fratelli:

To process your loan, we need a completed application as soon as possible. Please send the completed form to the loan processor along with copies (do not send originals) of the following documents:

- your last two years' tax returns

- your most recent pay stubs

On the application form, please complete the following items:

Item 3   Describe the purpose of the loan and enter the amount requested.

Item 4   List the balances on your bank accounts (4A). Enter the name and address of the institution and the account number. List any Certificates of Deposit, stocks, etc., as shown. (4B, 4C, and 4D).

Item 6C   If you have been at your current job for less than two years, enter the name and address of your previous employers. Include an explanation of any gap in employment during the past ten years.

Item 12A   Enter the name and address of the lender who holds your second deed of trust.

Item 16   List the current balances on all your credit cards (16B), outstanding loans (16C), and automobile loans (16D).

Item 23   Sign and date the form.

Please let me know if you have questions.

Sincerely,

Guidelines for Using Lists

Lists are more effective than paragraphs because they:

- communicate information more quickly

- save valuable writing time

- reduce the chance of grammar and punctuation errors

You can—and usually should—use a list whenever you present three or more related pieces of information. To make sure your lists are easy to read, follow the guidelines below.

1. **Use neutral symbols to mark items and leave space between items**

   Unnecessary numbers and letters tend to be distracting, because the text is already full of them.

   Use numbers only when you need them to indicate priority (such as the steps in a procedure). Use Arabic numbers (1, 2, 3), not Roman numerals (I, II, III).

   Unless you need numerals or letters, use neutral symbols such as "bullets" (•) to mark the items in lists.

   To avoid confusion about where an item starts and stops, leave at least one blank line between items.

   NOTE If items are only a few words, omit the blank line if you wish. But you must include it if any item is more than one line long, as in the examples on the next page.

ORIGINAL

The project team needs the following for the
quarterly meeting:

(A.) A conference room that will accommodate 30
      people seated six to a table
(B.) An overhead projector and screen
(C.) A VCR and monitor
(D.) A catered lunch

REVISION

The project team needs the following for the
quarterly meeting:

• A conference room that will accommodate 30
  people seated six to a table

• An overhead projector and screen

• A VCR and monitor

• A catered lunch

2. Only use end punctuation when at least one item contains more than one complete sentence.

In paragraphs, end punctuation (periods and question marks) tells readers when one sentence stops and another starts.

In lists, end punctuation is only necessary if an item contains more than one sentence. That's because the format of a list clearly shows where one item stops and another begins.

It's not wrong to use end punctuation. But if you use it for one item, you must use it for all items.

END PUNCTUATION UNNECESSARY

> We are unable to meet the original deadline for the following reasons:
>
> - Two team members resigned in October and we have been unable to replace them
>
> - The client expanded the project scope
>
> - Three weeks of heavy rain made it impossible to complete our investigation

END PUNCTUATION NECESSARY

> Here is a summary of our findings:
>
> - The costs of moving to a new location will be higher than we originally estimated. According to the most current figures, the total cost will exceed $150,000.
>
> - If we delay the move for five years, we will need an additional 10,000 square feet of space.
>
> - Only 30 percent of our employees say they would be willing to move out of California. Over 60 percent, however, would be willing to consider a move within the northern area of the state.

3. Introduce a list with a statement that tells readers what the list is about

> To express our appreciation for your business, we would like to offer you a choice of the following thank-you gifts:
>
> ☐ A 10% discount on purchases during May
>
> ☐ A discount coupon for the Milano Restorante
>
> ☐ A complimentary bottle of our best olive oil

4. Make sure the items in the list are parallel

The items in a list must be parallel — presented in the same form. For example, if one item begins with a verb, all the items must begin with verbs. If one item is a complete sentence, all the items must be complete sentences.

NOT PARALLEL

> The agenda for the March meeting includes:
> - discussion of the new health plan
> - whether to revise the procedures manual
> - drafting an early-retirement policy

PARALLEL

> The agenda for the March meeting includes:
> - discussing the new health plan
> - deciding whether to revise the procedures manual
> - drafting an early-retirement policy

5. Organize the list for your readers

Lists that include more than five or six items can be difficult to follow. Make lists easier to read by organizing the items into main points and subpoints.

TOO MANY ITEMS

Please supply the following for the conference that begins on October 22:

- 30 writing tablets for each meeting room
- 5 laptop computers for the community room
- an overhead projector for each meeting room
- coffee, tea, and pastry in the foyer each morning
- four six-foot round tables for each meeting room
- at least five telephones with outside lines in the community room
- a basket of fruit for each table in the meeting rooms
- a registration table in the foyer

ITEMS ORGANIZED

Please supply the following for the conference that begins on October 22:

In each meeting room
- 30 writing tablets
- an overhead projector
- four six-foot round tables
- a basket of fruit for each table

In the community room
- 5 laptop computers
- at least five telephones with outside lines

In the foyer
- coffee, tea, and pastry each morning
- a registration table

TRY IT   Use the space below or a blank sheet of paper to rewrite this paragraph into list form. Remember to include an introductory statement that tells readers what the list is about and establishes the context.

The task force found that the customer service representatives need training in how to respond to problems and complaints. There is widespread unhappiness about the quality of food in the cafeteria, indicating the need to find another vendor. How to implement flexible hours without creating logistical problems requires additional study. Finally, field representatives need more powerful laptop computers, which have not been included in this year's budget. These are the primary areas of concern the members of the task force believe they need to address during the next six months.

REVISION

_____

_____

_____

_____

_____

_____

_____

_____

_____

_____

Here are two ways to revise that paragraph into a list:

REVISION 1

Below are the primary areas of concern the members
of the task force believe they need to address
during the next six months:

- The customer service representatives need
  training in how to respond to problems and
  complaints

- There is widespread unhappiness about the
  quality of food in the cafeteria, indicating the
  need to find another vendor

- Additional study is needed to determine how to
  implement flexible hours without creating
  logistical problems

- Field representatives need more powerful laptop
  computers, which have not been included in this
  year's budget

REVISION 2

The task force members believe they must do the
following during the next six months:

- Train customer service representatives on ways
  to respond to problems and complaints

- Search for a new vendor who will improve the
  quality of food in the cafeteria

- Study ways to implement flexible hours without
  creating logistical problems

- Find funds to provide field representatives with
  the more powerful laptop computers they need

Try it one more time. Use the space below or a blank sheet of paper to revise this paragraph into a list.

> To help us update our database, please review the enclosed listings and notify us of any changes. First, proofread each listing and indicate any necessary corrections. Then please enter the best address for clients to reach you and at the same time verify that the telephone and fax numbers and Email addresses are correct. Finally, if you wish, you may add a maximum of two lines of explanation to each listing.

REVISION

_____

_____

_____

_____

_____

_____

_____

_____

_____

_____

_____

Here's one way to present the information more effectively. Your version might differ.

To help us update our database, please review the enclosed listings for the following and notify us of any changes:

- Proofread each listing and indicate any necessary corrections

- Enter the best address for clients to reach you

- Verify that telephone and fax numbers and Email addresses are correct

- If you wish, add a maximum of two lines of explanation to each listing

---

Now you know about openings, transitions and lists. Next, take a look at how to write an effective closing.

Closing Paragraphs

A strong closing:

■ makes a final personal contact with readers, most important when you're writing to influence

■ may restate the main point — what readers should do or know

■ wraps up any loose ends

■ tells readers clearly what happens next

■ uses specific language

Compare these two closings. Which do you prefer?

CLOSING 1	It would be appreciated if this situation could be rectified in a timely manner. Any questions can be addressed to this writer at the above address.
CLOSING 2	Please do whatever you can to locate the missing file by June 15. If I can help in any way, please call me at (415) 459-6712.

You probably preferred Closing 2. The first closing is impersonal and vague. The second is specific to the situation and conveys useful information.

Here are examples of the kinds of tired cliches that sound as if they were produced by a machine rather than by a person. You probably have seen similar closings many times.

Please contact the undersigned regarding time constraints on this policy.

Your assistance and cooperation will be greatly appreciated.

Do not hesitate to contact this writer should you require additional information.

Minor changes can transform those closings by making them **specific** to the piece of writing.

INSTEAD OF . . .   **TRY THIS . . .**

INSTEAD OF . . .	TRY THIS . . .
Please contact the above regarding time constraints on this policy.	Please call John Alcotts about the expiration date on this policy.
Your assistance and cooperation will be greatly appreciated.	I will be grateful for any help you can give me in tracking down the correct phone number.
Do not hesitate to contact this writer should you require additional information.	If you need a map or specific directions, please let me know.

PRACTICE

Write a closing for this letter.

Dear Mr. Hogan:

Thank you for asking about our new Flexible Loan
Program. I'm happy to send a brochure that
describes the program and includes an
application.

We designed this program after many discussions
with customers about what types of lending
arrangements they wanted. I think you'll find it
offers some unique ways of meeting your
financial needs.

_____

_____

_____

_____

_____

_____

_____

_____

| ANSWER TO PRACTICE |

Here is the type of closing you might have written:

```
Dear Mr. Hogan:

Thank you for asking about our new Flexible Loan
Program. I'm happy to send a brochure that
describes the program and includes an
application.

We designed this program after many discussions
with customers about what types of lending
arrangements they wanted. I think you'll find it
offers some unique ways of meeting your
financial needs.

Please let me know if you have questions about
this loan program. Otherwise, I'll call in two
weeks to see if you'd like to apply for a loan
under this new program.
```

Review

Fill in the blanks with the correct word or phrase. If you're not sure what to write, turn to the page number in the parentheses to the right of the sentence.

1. Before starting to write the first draft, always

    _____ your writing plan.   (85)

2. An effective opening:

    ■ makes a _____ contact with

    the _____

    ■ catches the reader's _____

    ■ includes a key sentence that tells the reader what you are

    _____ _____

    ■ is no more than _____ or

    _____ sentences long   (87)

    ■ Use transitions to _____ your
      ideas.   (94)

3. A strong closing:

    ■ makes a final _____

    _____ with readers

    ■ may _____ the main point

    ■ wraps up any _____ _____

    ■ tells readers clearly what _____ _____

    ■ uses _____ language   (111)

    _____

    Now turn the page for an assignment.

ASSIGNMENT

It's time to try out everything you've learned about writing your first draft.

You're going to draft a memo or letter, using the writing plan you completed at the end of Lesson 2.

OPTION   If you wish, you may start with a new situation. But **be sure to use a new Writing Worksheet to develop a new writing plan**. Please don't ignore everything you've learned so far by starting a draft without a plan.

What's Next?

In the next lesson you will learn how to use language that communicates clearly.

LESSON 4.
USING LANGUAGE THAT COMMUNICATES CLEARLY

LESSON 4
Using Language That Communicates Clearly

Introduction

Language should convey a message swiftly and accurately. Sometimes, however, language gets in the way of the message.

Sometimes writers use overly complicated language and sentence constructions to impress their readers. They lose sight of the fact that the most impressive thing a writer can do is convey ideas quickly, easily and so clearly that there is no chance for misunderstanding.

OBJECTIVES   In this lesson, you'll learn to use:

- Active language

- Specific language

- Plain English

- Real words

WHAT YOU NEED

- a dictionary

- a thesaurus

- a writing tablet

- a pen or pencil

- samples of your writing

Here is a letter in language so vague, pompous and passive that it's hard to tell just what the writer wants to say.

Dear Ms. Ellensby:

This is in reference to your recent letter which has been received and forwarded to the appropriate department for processing.

Please be advised that your complaint will be prioritized immediately and you will be contacted when the nature of the difficulty has been ascertained. Action will then be taken in accordance with the facts.

We regret this unfortunate occurrence. Please do not hesitate to contact this writer if further assistance is required.

Very sincerely yours,

Hard to follow, isn't it? Here's what the writer may have meant.

Dear Ms. Ellensby:

We are sorry that your loan documents were misplaced and the loan approval delayed.

I have asked Ms. Seto, Manager of our Research Department, to search for the documents immediately and report to me within three days. I will call you by next Friday to bring you up to date on the status of your application.

Sincerely,

The revised letter is easier to understand because the writer used active, specific, clear language.

To write clearly, use:

- active language

- specific language

- plain English

- real words instead of jargon

Use Active Language

Active language attracts the reader's attention and communicates directly and powerfully. On the other hand, passive language can weaken writing, confuse readers and make sentences longer.

In active language, the **actor** comes before the **action**.

ACTIVE   John *managed* the project.
(actor) (action)

PASSIVE   The project *was managed* by John.

To use active language, say **WHO** acted, not just what was done.

ACTIVE   *The team completed* the design document.

PASSIVE   The design document *has been completed*.

ACTIVE   *The committee prepared* a safety plan and *distributed* it to employees.

PASSIVE   A safety plan *was prepared* and *distributed* to employees.

By using active language, you write tighter sentences that are easier to understand.

When giving instructions, it is particularly important to say clearly what you want readers to do instead of writing passively and hinting at the action.

ACTIVE

(You) *Measure* the amount of water every 35 minutes.

—OR—

The technician should measure the amount of water every 35 minutes.

PASSIVE

The amount of water *should be measured* every 35 minutes.

The following examples show how to revise a passive sentence.

PASSIVE

The door *was found* unlocked three times during the past month.

ACTIVE

The security guard found the door unlocked three times during the past month.

PASSIVE

It *would be appreciated* if the report could be on my desk by noon on Monday.

ACTIVE

I *would appreciate your getting* the report to me by noon on Monday.

—OR—

Please deliver the report to me by noon on Monday.

**Now, turn the page for some practice
changing passive language to active.**

PRACTICE

Revise these sentences so they are **active** and **direct.**

❖ **HINT**   The first step is to identify (or make up) an **actor.**

The research project is being conducted by the News Department.

_____

_____

_____

_____

A copy of the approval must be stapled to the request before it is forwarded to the Accounting Office.

_____

_____

_____

_____

The new design is attached for your review and its return by March 15 would be appreciated.

_____

_____

_____

_____

An investigation will be conducted by Andrea Carelli into the complaint made by Mr. Szabo.

_____

_____

_____

_____

Reservations for the conference can be made by telephoning Tom Woo at Extension 4732 before December 1.

_____

_____

_____

_____

Check your answers on the next page.

ANSWERS TO PRACTICE

Your revisions may not be identical to these, but they should be similar. The important thing is to be sure the **actor** comes before the action.

ORIGINAL   The research project is being conducted by the News Department.

REVISION   *The News Department is conducting* the Research Project.

ORIGINAL   A copy of the approval must be stapled to the request before it is forwarded to the Accounting Office.

REVISION   *You must staple* a copy of the approval to the request before *forwarding* it to the Accounting Office.

—OR—

Staple a copy of the approval to the request before *you forward* it to the Accounting Office.

ORIGINAL   The new design is attached for your review and its return by March 15 would be appreciated.

REVISION   Please *review* the design and *return* it by March 15.

—OR—

REVISION   *I've attached* the new design for your review and *would appreciate your returning* it by March 15.

ORIGINAL   An investigation will be conducted by Andrea Carelli into the complaint made by Mr. Szabo.

REVISION   *Andrea Carelli will investigate* Mr. Szabo's complaint.

ORIGINAL   Reservations for the conference can be made by telephoning Tom Woo at Extension 4732 before December 1.

REVISION   *To make* reservations for the conference, *telephone* Tom Woo at Extension 4732 before December 1.

—OR—

You can make reservations for the conference by *telephoning* Tom Woo at Extension 4732 before December 1.

ASSIGNMENT

Do you use too much passive language when you write? Take a look at your own writing — the drafts you completed earlier in this program or any other writing samples you may have.

You will probably find at least a few passive, indirect sentences. Write two of them below, then revise the sentences so they are active and direct. (If you don't find any passive sentences, go on to the next section of this lesson.)

ORIGINAL   _____

_____

_____

_____

REVISION   _____

_____

_____

_____

ORIGINAL   _____

_____

_____

_____

REVISION   _____

_____

_____

_____

Use Specific Language

Another way to make your writing easier to read is by using **specific** language. The more precise and specific your language, the more information you give readers and the easier it is for them to understand your message.

Here are a few examples:

VAGUE The *building* was *destroyed* in a *disaster some time ago.*

SPECIFIC *Fire* destroyed the *apartment house* in *1964.*

VAGUE Our *group went* to Los Angeles for a *meeting.*

SPECIFIC Our *project team flew* to Los Angeles to *meet with Harriet Alan, the system designer.*

VAGUE Have the client *complete* the *paperwork* in a *timely manner.*

SPECIFIC Ask the client to *fill out the new account application form and signature card within ten working days.*

To make your writing less abstract, use **specific words**. The more specific a word or phrase, the fewer things it names and, consequently, the more precise information it conveys:

GENERAL ⟶	SPECIFIC
vehicle	car
car	sedan
equipment	computer
computer	laptop
went	walked, ran, drove
traveled	flew, took the train, sailed
contacted	called, spoke to, visited
proper	correct, easy-to-use
some	four or five
recently	yesterday
in a timely manner	by August 15, within two weeks

PRACTICE

Underline the vague, general words and phrases in these sentences. Then use your imagination to fill in details and revise the sentences so they communicate specific, useful information.

Recently, we looked at a structure that might be suitable for our needs.

_____

_____

_____

During the incident, Ms. Brown sustained multiple injuries to her upper torso and limbs.

_____

_____

_____

We have identified a few items to be discussed at the meeting, so please leave considerable time in your schedule.

_____

_____

_____

ANSWERS TO PRACTICE

These are possible revisions. Yours will be different because you used different details. You should have noticed, however, that the italicized words are vague and imprecise and chosen more concrete terms.

ORIGINAL   *Recently*, we looked at a *structure* that might be *suitable* for our *needs*.

REVISION   Last week we found a four-story building that might be big enough for our new machine polishers.

ORIGINAL   During the *incident*, Ms. Brown *sustained multiple injuries* to her *upper torso* and *limbs*.

REVISION   During the riot, Ms. Brown's chest, shoulders and arms were scratched and cut. Her right wrist was broken.

ORIGINAL   We have identified *a few items* to be discussed at the meeting, so please leave *considerable time* in your schedule.

REVISION   At the meeting, we will discuss the next conference, the move to the new building, and the new staff position, so please leave at least three hours in your schedule.

ASSIGNMENT

Check your own writing to see whether you use vague, general words and phrases. Circle any examples you find. Write two of them below and change the words or phrases so they are more specific.

ORIGINAL _____

_____

_____

REVISION _____

_____

_____

ORIGINAL _____

_____

_____

REVISION _____

_____

_____

Use Plain English

Do you ever have to re-read something or read it very slowly because the writer used language more formal than the situation warranted? These **pompous** words and phrases force readers to translate what they're reading into everyday language—and that's a waste of valuable time.

EXAMPLE   How many times do you have to read this paragraph to be sure you understand it?

> Per your request, enclosed herewith are documents concerning the above mentioned project. Please review said documents and return them to this office prior to January 1. We will then initiate the process of implementing the requested modifications.

See how much easier the paragraph is to read when it's written in **plain English**:

> As you asked, I'm sending a description of the Acme project. Please read the description and send it back to me before January 15. We'll then start making the system changes.

Pompous language never helps communication. Nor does it impress readers. Instead, it gets in the way of your message.

So when you write, use standard language—**plain English**. Choose words that communicate your message as precisely, simply and directly as possible.

PRACTICE

Sometimes the words on the left are the best ones to use. But writers often use them when simpler, more direct words would communicate more clearly. What if they're really too pompous for the situation? What words or phrases can you use instead? Use your thesaurus or dictionary if you're not sure.

prior to _____

subsequent to _____

utilize _____

modifications _____

enhance _____

beneficial _____

supplemental _____

magnitude _____

supersede _____

augment _____

heretofore _____

herein _____

parameters _____

commence _____

to endeavor _____

optimal _____

ANSWERS TO PRACTICE

These are possible answers. Yours need not be identical.

prior to	before
subsequent to	after, following
utilize	use
modifications	changes
enhance	improve
beneficial	helpful
supplemental	extra
magnitude	size
supersede	replace
augment	increase, add to
heretofore	before, until now
herein	in
parameters	boundaries, limits
commence	start, begin
to endeavor	to try
optimal	best, most favorable

| PRACTICE |

Revise these sentences into **plain English.** Also, you will probably want to revise the sentences into active language.

Division managers are herewith requested to facilitate the implementation of the aforementioned program by forwarding copies of their personnel requirements.

_____

_____

_____

_____

The injuries sustained by the passenger during the accident were the result of his failure to use the vehicle's restraining retentioning elements.

_____

_____

_____

_____

Enclosed herewith is a listing of procedures that must be implemented immediately.

_____

_____

_____

_____

ANSWERS TO PRACTICE

Your revisions might look something like these.

REVISION   Please help us get this program started by letting us know how many people you need to complete the job.

—OR—

To get this program off the ground, Division managers must send us a list of their personnel needs.

REVISION   The passenger was injured during the accident because he didn't use the seat belt.

—OR—

The passenger's injuries were a result of his failure to use a seat belt.

REVISION   Here is a list of procedures that must be put into operation immediately.

—OR—

Please begin using these procedures at once.

ASSIGNMENT

Look for examples of **pompous** language in your own writing. If you find any, write them below. On the revision lines, rewrite the sentences into plain English.

ORIGINAL
_____

_____

_____

_____

REVISION
_____

_____

_____

_____

ORIGINAL
_____

_____

_____

_____

REVISION
_____

_____

_____

_____

**Next, look at the importance of using
real words when you write.**

Use Real Words

Webster's *New Collegiate Dictionary* defines **jargon** as:

> . . . . a hybrid language or dialect simplified in vocabulary and used for communication between specific people. . . . the technical terminology or characteristic idiom of a special activity or group. . . .

Business writing is full of words, phrases, abbreviations and acronyms that make sense only to members of a certain group. People outside that group may not understand such terms or may use them in a different way.

To communicate clearly, it's important to avoid jargon, made-up words, and obscure or incorrect forms of ordinary words that your readers might not easily understand.

Here are some examples of language to avoid:

REAL WORDS USED INCORRECTLY

We have started a new campaign to **migrate** customers to our bank.

WORDS YOU WON'T FIND IN THE DICTIONARY (at least not yet)

We hope to achieve **maximalization** of our marketing potential.

ACRONYMS

Next year's goals include increasing the **BOCSF**, establishing a new **RADIT**, and improving the current **FAJ**.

To see how difficult it is to understand other people's jargon, try to define these words and acronyms. It's okay to guess.

cash cow

_____

_____

rightsizing

_____

_____

annualized

_____

_____

cobweb site

_____

_____

YODA

_____

_____

COO

_____

_____

pharming

_____

_____

permalancer

_____

_____

Here's what we understand the words and acronyms to mean. You may have come up with other meanings. When it comes to jargon, there are no wrong answers.

cash cow	A business that brings in a lot of money
rightsizing	Reducing the workforce
annualized	Happening every year
cobweb site	An outdated internet site
YODA	"Young Opinionated Directionless Artistes"
COO	"Chief Operating Officer"
pharming	The process of genetically engineering farm products
permalancer	A permanent freelancer

**Did you have trouble defining the words and phrases?
If so, you can sympathize with readers faced
with jargon they can't understand.**

ASSIGNMENT

Each type of business has its own jargon—it's easier to pick out other people's jargon than to recognize jargon you use daily.

Occasionally, jargon is a quick, easy way of getting your message across. But not all readers will understand it. So it's important to recognize the jargon you use and be able to translate it into real words.

Look for examples of jargon in your own writing. If you find any, write the words below and then translate the jargon into real words.

JARGON   **TRANSLATION**

_____   _____

_____   _____

_____   _____

_____   _____

_____   _____

_____   _____

_____   _____

_____

Review

Fill in the blanks with the correct word or phrase. If you're not sure, check the page number to the right of the sentence.

1. In active language, the _____ comes first,

    then the _____.   (120)

2. The more specific a word or phrase, the

    _____ things it names.   (128)

3. Pompous words force readers to _____

    what they're reading into _____
    language.   (132)

4. Business writing is full of words, phrases, abbreviations

    and acronyms that _____

    _____ .   (138)

What's Next?

In this lesson, you've examined ways of using language to communicate more actively, precisely and clearly. Next, you'll look at ways to write more **concisely** by eliminating words that serve no purpose.

LESSON 5.
USING CONCISE LANGUAGE

LESSON 5
Using Concise Language

Introduction

A common obstacle to good business writing is unnecessary words. This clutter slows readers down. It can also make writing tedious and boring.

By eliminating unnecessary words, you make it easier for readers to get your message and your writing will be more interesting to read.

OBJECTIVES   In this lesson, you'll learn to write more concisely by:

- Identifying and eliminating unnecessary words

WHAT YOU NEED

- a writing tablet
- a pen or pencil
- samples of your writing

Identifying Clutter

It's not the number of words that's the problem — it's the number of **unnecessary** words. You want to use only those words that help the reader understand what you are saying. If a word or phrase is not useful, get rid of it.

Here are a few examples of clutter — words that just take up space. Which words do you think are unnecessary?

EXAMPLES

- His inventory was large in size.

- Please let me know as to whether you will attend the party.

- The noise levels of the trains arriving and departing from the station are relatively low by what are considered to be current standards of the present rapid transit industry.

- There are several employees who want to take vacations in June.

Here are the words you could easily eliminate:

- His inventory was large~~, in size.~~

- Please let me know ~~as to~~ whether you will attend the party.

- The noise levels of the (trains) arriving and departing ~~from the station~~ are relatively low by ~~what are considered to be~~ current standards ~~of the present rapid transit industry~~.

- ~~There are~~ Several employees ~~who~~ want to take vacations in June.

In this lesson, you'll look at several ways to get rid of clutter. After reading each set of examples, you'll practice revising wordy sentences. Then you'll review your own writing to see if you can get rid of any words that interfere with your message.

Here are three ways you can reduce clutter:

- Use only one word for a one-word idea

- Avoid repetitions

- Eliminate unnecessary "there are," "who," "that" and "which" clauses

Use Only One Word for a One-Word Idea

EXAMPLE	She solved the problem in a clever way.
REVISION	She solved the problem ~~in a clever way.~~ *cleverly*

—OR—

She *cleverly* solved the problem ~~in a clever way.~~

EXAMPLE	We are in agreement with you about the contract terms.
REVISION	We ~~are in~~ agree~~ment~~ with you about the contract terms.

Try some practice on the next page.

PRACTICE

Revise these sentences to eliminate unnecessary phrases.

EXAMPLE   The client visited the site ~~of the~~ project on May 15.

She drove in a reckless manner.

We conducted a survey of the members.

The manager made an offer to buy everyone coffee.

I believe this procedure will make an improvement in the way reports are filed.

He called us with regard to his recent insurance claim.

Due to the fact that she had been drinking, the accident was her fault.

We requested he appear in person for the purpose of testifying in his own defense.

Check your answers on the next page.

ANSWERS TO PRACTICE

Your answers should be similar to these.

She drove ~~in a reckless manner~~ recklessly.

We ~~conducted a~~ survey**ed** ~~of~~ the members.

The manager ~~made an~~ offer**ed** to buy everyone coffee.

I believe this procedure will ~~make an improvement in~~ **improve** the way reports are filed.

He called us ~~with regard to~~ **about** his recent insurance claim.

Because ~~Due to the fact that~~ she had been drinking, the accident was her fault.

We requested he appear ~~for the purpose of~~ **to** testify~~ing~~ in his own defense.

Avoid Repetitions

EXAMPLES

alternative choices	important essentials
basic fundamentals	end result
serious crisis	future plans
final outcome	separate entities
past experience	advance warning
surrounding circumstances	two equal halves
equally as effective as	regular weekly meetings
symptoms indicative of	absolutely complete
desirable benefits	ten a.m. in the morning

PRACTICE   Eliminate the obvious repetitions in these sentences.

The urban residents of the city are unhappy with the new tax.

The subterranean garage, located underground, is more secure than the old one.

Until last week, our group had the best record to date.

ANSWERS TO PRACTICE

Your revisions should resemble these:

The ~~urban~~ residents ~~of the~~ (city) are unhappy with the new tax.

—OR—

The urban residents ~~of the city~~ are unhappy with the new tax.

The subterranean garage, ~~located underground,~~ is more secure than the old one.

Until last week, our group had the best record ~~to date.~~

—OR—

~~Until last week,~~ Our group had the best record to date.

Eliminate Unnecessary "There are," "Who," "That," and "Which" Clauses

EXAMPLE	There are several applicants who have the background for this position.
REVISION	~~There are~~ Several applicants ~~who~~ have the background for this position.
EXAMPLE	The broker who works in Chicago sent the file which is incomplete to the home office.
REVISION	The broker ~~who works in Chicago~~ sent the file ~~which is~~ incomplete to the home office.

PRACTICE Revise these sentences by eliminating the unnecessary clauses.

The members of your group who are interested in learning more about this software are welcome to attend the demonstration that will be conducted on February 16.

There are thousands of hours wasted because no one can use the files which are out of date.

The topic for the next luncheon meeting, which will be held on January 1, is "Literacy in the Workplace."

ANSWERS TO PRACTICE

Your revisions should be similar to these.

The members of your group ~~who are~~ interested in learning more about this software are welcome to attend the demonstration ~~that will be conducted on February 16.~~

~~There are~~ thousands of hours *are* wasted because no one can use the (files) ~~which are~~ out-of-date.

The topic for the ~~next~~ luncheon meeting, ~~which will be held on (January 1)~~, is "Literacy in the Workplace."

—OR—

The topic for the next luncheon meeting, ~~which will be held~~ on January 1, is "Literacy in the Workplace."

PRACTICE

Here's the chance to pull together what you've learned so far. These sentences have a variety of "clutter" problems. Keeping in mind all the types of clutter, revise the sentences so they are concise.

On the basis of your recent letter, I would like to take this opportunity to inform you that I will investigate the problem about the delay in processing your loan which you mentioned and send you a letter in order to report my findings.

At this point in time, it is our understanding that the new computer system will have the capability of processing 50 percent more information than the amount which is processed by our present system.

With regard to the current status of your request for additional office equipment, we have submitted an "Addition to Budget" request for the purpose of obtaining the funds that are needed to initiate the purchase.

Check your answers on the next page.

Your revisions should be similar to the ones below and on the facing page.

~~On the basis of your recent letter,~~ I would like to ~~take this opportunity to~~ inform you that I will investigate ~~the problem about~~ the delay in processing your loan ~~which you mentioned~~ and ~~send you a letter in order to~~ report my findings.

—OR—

~~On the basis of~~ [Thank you for] ~~your~~ ~~recent~~ letter. ~~I would like to take this opportunity to inform you that~~ I will investigate ~~the problem about~~ the delay in processing your loan ~~which you mentioned,~~ and send you a letter ~~in order to report~~ [with] my findings.

~~At this point in time, it is our~~ [we] understand~~ing that~~ the new computer system will ~~have the capability of~~ [be able to] process~~ing~~ 50 percent more information~~than the amount which is processed by our present system.~~

—OR—

At this ~~point in~~ time, [we] ~~it is our~~ understand~~ing that~~ the new computer system will ~~have the capability of~~ [be able to] process~~ing~~ 50 percent more information than ~~the amount which is processed by~~ our present system.

~~With regard to the current status of your request for~~
~~additional office equipment,~~ ~~W~~e have submitted an
"Addition to Budget" request ~~for the purpose of~~
_to_ obtain~~ing~~ the funds ~~that are needed~~ to ~~initiate the~~
purchase∧ additional office equipment.

—OR—

With regard to ~~the current status of~~ your request for
additional office equipment, we have submitted an
"Addition to Budget" request ~~for the purpose of~~
_to_ obtain~~ing~~ the∧ _necessary_ funds ~~that are needed to initiate the~~
~~purchas~~e.

**You are probably getting very good at spotting and eliminating
clutter. Turn the page for one last practice before
looking at your own writing for unnecessary words.**

PRACTICE

Revise these paragraphs to make sure they are as concise as possible without changing the meaning. Indicate your changes right on this page. You do not have to recopy the letter.

During the month of March, the people who are working on the HUF project made a study of the past history of HUF in order to come to some conclusions as to whether the proper analyses were made for the purpose of determining the Project goals.

The people who were members of this study group are of the opinion that the original analysis was done in a hasty manner and there were several errors in the original conclusions. At this point in time, it appears that the main problem is a matter of making a decision as to whether to still continue the Project or to undertake and perform a new analysis.

We have enclosed for your information the details which resulted from the study. Due to the fact that time is a factor in this situation, we would greatly appreciate your prompt review of the information and your decision.

_____

Check your revisions on the next page.

ANSWERS TO PRACTICE

Your revisions should be similar.

During ~~the month of~~ March, ~~the people who are working on~~ the HUF project ^team studied ~~made a study of the~~ ^HUF'S ~~past~~ history ~~of HUF in order~~ to ^determine ~~come to some conclusions as to~~ whether the proper analyses were made ~~for the purpose of~~ ^when determining ~~the~~ Project goals.

The ~~people who were~~ members of this study group ^believe ~~are of the opinion that~~ the original analysis was done ^hastily ~~in a hasty manner~~ and there were several errors in the ~~original~~ conclusions. At this ~~point in~~ time, it appears ~~that~~ the main problem is ~~a matter of~~ making a decision ^about ~~as to~~ whether to ~~still~~ continue the Project or to undertake ~~and perform~~ a new analysis.

We have enclosed ~~for your information the details which resulted from~~ the study ^results⊙ ~~Due to the fact that~~ ^Because time is a factor, ~~in this situation,~~ we would ~~greatly~~ appreciate your prompt ~~review of the information and your~~ decision.

Review

To review what you've learned in this lesson, answer these questions.

1. To write concisely, use only those words that help

   _____

   _____ (145)

2. To reduce clutter:

   ■ use only _____ _____ for a one-word idea

   ■ avoid _____

   eliminate unnecessary " _____ _____,"

   "_____," "_____" and

   "_____" clauses. (146)

Read one or more of your writing samples. Select two or three sentences you think are the most cluttered and write them below. Then revise the sentences so they are concise.

ORIGINAL   _____

_____

_____

_____

REVISION   _____

_____

_____

_____

ORIGINAL   _____

_____

_____

_____

REVISION   _____

_____

_____

_____

ORIGINAL

_____

_____

_____

_____

REVISION

_____

_____

_____

_____

What's Next?

You have completed this lesson. In Lesson 6, you'll examine sentence structure and review some principles of grammar and punctuation.

LESSON 6.
USING CORRECT SENTENCE STRUCTURE,
PUNCTUATION AND GRAMMAR

L E S S O N   6
Using Correct Sentence Structure, Punctuation and Grammar

Introduction

Writing errors can confuse readers. Equally important, errors are unprofessional.

In this lesson you'll review some rules for sentence structure, punctuation and grammar, focusing on areas that seem to cause the most problems for people who write business documents.

OBJECTIVES   In this lesson, you'll learn to write clearly and professionally by:

■ Editing your writing for correct sentence structure, punctuation and grammar

WHAT YOU NEED

■ a writing tablet

■ a pen or pencil

■ samples of your writing

**Begin by looking at common problems
with sentence structure.**

Sentence Structure

Sometimes a sentence is hard to understand because it is:

■ too long

■ a run-on sentence containing clauses that are connected incorrectly

SENTENCES THAT ARE TOO LONG

A common problem is a sentence that is too long to comprehend in one reading. Studies show that people generally have to read sentences of more than 28-30 words at least twice.

How many times do you have to read this sentence?

```
To help Debra succeed in her present position, we
recommend that she be given the opportunity to
participate with the department supervisor, in
meetings to be held twice a month starting in the
first quarter of next year, with the specific
purpose of discussing alternative work methods for
processing work flow. (51)
```

See how much easier these shorter sentences are to follow:

```
To help Debra succeed in her present position, we
recommend that she be given the opportunity to
participate in meetings with her supervisor. (23)
These meetings will be held twice a month starting
in the first quarter of next year. (16) During
these meetings, Debra and her supervisor can
discuss alternative methods for processing work
flow. (15)
```

As a general rule, keep the average length of your sentences to 17–24 words, with only one or two thoughts per sentence. If you are using technical or unusual terms, drop the count to 15–18 words.

Here's how to determine if your sentences are too long:

- Count the number of words in each of five consecutive sentences. Include small words such as "a," "the," "to," etc.

- Divide the total by five.

EXAMPLE

> The Data Processing Group has failed to meet its schedules for the past six months, causing delays and confusion throughout the organization. (22) To remedy this situation, please make sure all team members follow the Data Processing Organizational Plan procedures to the letter. (20)
>
> The Plan, which was distributed to all the teams in November, clearly establishes objectives and priorities for all department projects. (20) The procedures it contains explain each team member's responsibilities in detail. (11) The procedures also provide steps to take in the case of problems. (12)

Words per sentence: 22 + 20 + 20 + 11 + 12 = 85

Average words per sentence: 85 ÷ 5 = 17

Now look at one of your writing samples.

Count the number of words in each of five consecutive sentences.

- Write down the number of words in each sentence:

  sentence 1 _____   sentence 4 _____

  sentence 2 _____   sentence 5 _____

  sentence 3 _____

- Add the five numbers and write the total _____

- Divide the total by five and write that number _____

If the average number of words per sentence is more than 25, pay closer attention to the length of your sentences.

Here is an easy method for revising a long sentence.

ORIGINAL SENTENCE

```
I worked with a number of managers and supervisors
to explore the issues which surfaced during the
change process, including concerns about their own
limitations, a sense of loss as a result of
change, reconciliation of conflicting needs and
priorities and how to preserve their own sense of
worth when everyone else seems to be moving
forward. (57)
```

1. List the ideas.

I worked with managers and supervisors to explore the issues resulting from changes. Issues included:

- concerns about their limitations
- sense of loss as a result of change
- concerns about conflicting needs and priorities
- ways to preserve their sense of self-worth

2. Write separate sentences containing only one or two ideas. Use transitions to link the sentences.

REVISED SENTENCE

```
I worked with a number of managers and supervisors
to explore the issues which surfaced during the
change process. (19)

Two of the major issues concerned feelings about
their own limitations and their sense of loss as a
result of change. (21) In addition, they wanted to
reconcile their conflicting needs and priorities.
(11) Finally, they are working to preserve their
own sense of self-worth when everyone else seems
to be moving forward. (19)
```

Now try some practice.

PRACTICE

Revise this 55-word sentence into several shorter ones.

> I have enclosed a survey form that will allow you to give me feedback about the process by which the display booth was set up to help us learn whether our customers were satisfied with the arrangements and if they were not, we want to know what specific changes we should make for next year.

1. List the ideas.

_____

_____

_____

_____

2. Write separate sentences containing only one or two ideas. Use transitions to link sentences.

_____

_____

_____

_____

_____

_____

_____

_____

Turn the page to check your revision.

ANSWER TO PRACTICE

Your revision should look something like this:

I have enclosed a survey form that will allow you to give me feedback about the process by which the display booth was set up. (25) Your feedback will help us learn whether our customers were satisfied with the arrangements. (14) If they were not satisfied, we want to know what specific changes we should make for next year. (18)

ASSIGNMENT

Review your own writing. Look for a sentence that is more than 24 words long. Write the original and the revision here. (If you don't find any, go on to the next section of this lesson.)

ORIGINAL
_____

_____

_____

_____

_____

REVISION
_____

_____

_____

_____

_____

_____

**Next, we'll look at another common
writing error — run-on sentences.**

RUN-ON SENTENCES

The second most common problem is the run-on sentence. A run-on sentence contains clauses that are connected incorrectly.

Run-on sentences result from combining two complete sentences without using:

- a connecting word such as "and," "but," "or," "nor," "for," "yet," or "so"

—AND/OR—

- the right punctuation

Here are the two most common forms of run-on sentences:

Two complete sentences joined only with a comma

Service calls are expensive, you can purchase a five-year service contract for $100.

Two complete sentences joined only with a comma and a word such as "however," "therefore," or "meanwhile"

Service calls are expensive, however, you can purchase a five-year service contract for $100.

Here are four ways to correct a run-on sentence:

Write two complete sentences.

> Service calls are expensive. You can purchase a five-year service contract for $100.

Use a comma and a connecting word such as "and," "but," "or," "nor," "for," "yet," or "so."

> Service calls are expensive, but you can purchase a five-year service contract for $100.

Use a semicolon.

> Service calls are expensive; you can purchase a five-year service contract for $100.

Use a semicolon and a word such as "however," "therefore," "meanwhile," "also," etc.

> Service calls are expensive; however, you can purchase a five-year service contract for $100.

Try some practice.

PRACTICE

Put an "X" next to the run-on sentences. Then use any of the methods explained earlier to correct them.

RUN-ON?

EXAMPLE   We met for six hours; however, we could not reach a consensus.

X

1. The agency completed the investigation last month; its findings were inconclusive.

_____

2. We believe the problem is a separate one, it is not related to the earlier fire.

_____

3. She has received the most up-to-date treatment, her recovery is hindered by her depression.

_____

4. Let me know if you would like to meet with our team; meanwhile, we will proceed with the project.

_____

5. We had hoped to make a decision by now, however, we are still waiting for information from the client.

_____

Check your answers on the next page.

ANSWERS TO PRACTICE

1. The agency completed the investigation last month; its findings were inconclusive.

    _____

2. We believe the problem is a separate one; it is not related to the earlier fire.

    X
    _____

3. She has received the most up-to-date treatment, **but** her recovery is hindered by her depression.

    X
    _____

4. Let me know if you would like to meet with our team; meanwhile, we will proceed with the project.

    _____

5. We had hoped to make a decision by now; however, we are still waiting for information from the client.

    X
    _____

ASSIGNMENT

Review your own writing samples for examples of run-on sentences. If you find any, write the originals and revisions here. If you don't find any, go on to the next section of this lesson.

ORIGINAL _____

_____

_____

_____

REVISION _____

_____

_____

_____

ORIGINAL _____

_____

_____

REVISION _____

_____

_____

_____

**Now that you know how to write shorter
sentences and correct run-on sentences,
it's time to look at punctuation.**

Punctuation

People often find punctuation rules confusing because there are so many of them and they do not always seem consistent. But if you keep your sentences short enough to read easily, you only need to think about a few rules.

In this section, you will review when and how to use these punctuation marks:

■ commas

■ semicolons

■ colons

THE COMMA

After periods, commas are the most frequently used punctuation marks. Although there are many times you might chose to use a comma, there are only four situations in which you must use a comma:

■ To prevent misunderstanding

■ To separate the numerals in dates and to separate the parts of an address

■ To set off a phrase or clause that is not essential to the meaning of the sentence

■ To separate words in a series

Use commas to prevent misunderstanding

See how easily a comma clears up the confusion in these sentences.

ORIGINAL   Although there were jobs for a hundred thousands applied.

REVISION   Although there were jobs for a hundred, thousands applied.

ORIGINAL   In brief the report will take about an hour.

REVISION   In brief, the report will take about an hour.

PRACTICE

Insert commas where you think necessary.

EXAMPLE   After all, the time he has taken has been well spent.

1. As you know nothing changed as a result of the investigation.

2. If you want to swim the pool is a block away.

3. To summarize case histories are the most important documents in our files.

Check your answers on the next page.

1. As you know, nothing changed as a result of the investigation.

2. If you want to swim, the pool is a block away.

3. To summarize, case histories are the most important documents in our files.

Use commas to separate the parts of a date or an address.

ORIGINAL   January 1 1988 was the date of the great flood.

REVISION   January 1, 1988, was the date of the great flood.

NOTE   When the date consists only of the month and year, you may omit the comma after the month.

EXAMPLE   He retired in June 1994.

ORIGINAL   He lived at 186 Elm Lane Hibbing Minnesota.

REVISION   He lived at 186 Elm Lane, Hibbing, Minnesota.

PRACTICE

Insert commas where you think necessary.

1. When the client died on September 28 1953 his policy was still pending.

2. We inspected the property at 230 Clark Street Novato California on May 1 1984 and found the leak had still not been repaired.

3. She has been with the company since July 1993.

Turn the page to check your answers.

ANSWERS TO PRACTICE

1. When the client died on September 28,1953,his policy was still pending.

2. We inspected the property at 230 Clark Street,Novato,California on May 1,1984,and found the leak had still not been repaired.

3. She has been with the company since July 1993.

—OR—

4. She has been with the company since July,1993.

Use commas to set off a phrase or clause that is not essential to the meaning of a sentence.

A clause modifies the subject of the sentence. See if you can underline the clause in this sentence:

I got the job through Mr. Clark, who is a family friend.

If you underlined *who is a family friend*, you recognize a clause.

Do *not* set off essential clauses with commas. A clause is essential if removing it changes the meaning of the sentence.

WITH CLAUSE	All cars *that have faulty brakes* should be kept off the streets.
WITHOUT CLAUSE	All cars should be kept off the streets.

The clause *that have faulty brakes* is essential. The sentence has a different meaning without the clause.

Use commas to set off clauses that are *not* essential.

A clause is not essential if removing it leaves the meaning of the sentence unchanged:

WITH CLAUSE   Dave's mother, *who is eighty-seven*, is coming to visit in July.

WITHOUT CLAUSE   Dave's mother is coming to visit in July.

In this example, removing the clause *who is eighty-seven* does not change the essential meaning of the sentence.

Again, here is the basic rule:

- ■ If removing a clause changes the meaning of the sentence, *do not* set it off with commas

- ■ If removing the clause leaves the meaning of the sentence unchanged, use commas to set it off

PRACTICE

Underline the clauses in these sentences. Then insert commas to set off clauses that can be removed without changing the meaning of the sentence.

1. Her memo which I received yesterday stated very clearly that the work was to be completed by next month.

2. Activities of our company that are directly related to this program are developed by the Processing Division.

3. Engineers who are new to this procedure should not try to carry it out themselves.

4. The report which was written by hand was submitted on time.

5. Our neighbor who lives in the green house did not return the lawn mower.

Check your answers on the next page.

ANSWERS TO PRACTICE

1. Her memo, <u>which I received yesterday</u>, stated very clearly that the work was to be completed by next month.

2. Activities of our company <u>that are directly related to this program</u> are developed by the Processing Division.

3. Engineers <u>who are new to this procedure</u> should not try to carry it out themselves.

4. The report, <u>which was written by hand</u>, was submitted on time.

5. Our neighbor, <u>who lives in the green house</u>, did not return the lawn mower.

Use commas to separate words in a series.

Writers usually remember to use a comma between words in a series. What they may not remember is whether they have to use one before the final item in the series.

Unless your organization has its own policy, you usually have a choice about whether to use a comma before the final item in a series. But always use the final, or "series," comma if the reader might be confused by its omission.

In Example 1, the series comma is optional. But in Example 2, the reader might be confused if the series comma is left out. The comma makes it clear that the buns go with the hamburgers and not with the ice cream.

EXAMPLE 1   He wrote up the policy, sent a copy to the client, and filed a bill.

—OR—

He wrote up the policy, sent a copy to the client and filed a bill.

EXAMPLE 2   He planned to serve crackers and cheese, hamburgers and buns, and ice cream and cake.

**Before practicing the use of commas in a series,
take a look at the colon and the semicolon.**

THE COLON

There are many situations in which you might use a colon. We're going to look at the three ways the colon is most commonly used in business writing.

Always use a colon after the salutation of a business letter.

EXAMPLE   Dear Ms. Young:

Use a colon to introduce a series.

EXAMPLES   There are three things you must know about your new job: starting hours, ending hours and vacations.

The new library needs these items:

- business newspapers

- trade magazines

- videotapes

- instructional materials

You can use a colon to introduce a statement, an example or a question.

EXAMPLES   I need the signed contract before we begin the project: no later than September 16 if you want us to start on the following Friday.

My manager has one crucial question: Is the system you described compatible with our existing system?

For business writing, you seldom need to use a colon in any other situation. But if you'd like to know more about how to use colons correctly, see the punctuation section in one of the reference books listed at the end of this program.

THE SEMICOLON

In business writing you can use a semicolon to:

- join two independent clauses when you do not want to use a coordinating conjunction such as "and," "but," etc.

- separate elements in a series that already contains commas

- join two independent clauses with a word such as "however," "therefore," etc.

EXAMPLES   They agreed to select the lowest bidder; they had to wait ten days for the results.

The group elected the following officers: Joe Lewis, treasurer; Bobette Jones, secretary; Louise Boswart, president; and Jose Clark, vice president.

We expected the report the first week of June; however, the project manager has asked for a two-week delay.

Turn the page for some practice.

PRACTICE

Write in colons, semicolons and/or commas where necessary.

1. The doctor said the condition had three symptoms fear and depression hives and itching and hunger and thirst.

2. The boys walked home from practice their coach had left without them.

3. There are three new team members Erin Copland pitcher Jennifer Fisher catcher and Pat Jonas shortstop.

4. I find the Sherwood proposition very appealing however I'd like to know more about the product before continuing.

5. I have one major concern about the Bensen survey why did they send questionnaires only to people who own car phones?

Turn the page and check your answers.

ANSWERS TO PRACTICE

1. The doctor said the condition had three symptoms: fear and depression, hives and itching, and hunger and thirst.

—OR—

The doctor said the condition had three symptoms: fear and depression; hives and itching; and hunger and thirst.

2. The boys walked home from practice; their coach had left without them.

3. There are three new team members: Erin Copland, pitcher; Jennifer Fisher, catcher; and Pat Jonas, shortstop.

4. I find the Sherwood proposition very appealing; however, I'd like to know more about the product before continuing.

5. I have one major concern about the Bensen survey: why did they send questionnaires only to people who own car phones?

_____

There's an assignment on the next page.

Review your own writing samples for incorrect use of commas, semi-colons and colons. If you see any errors, write the originals and revisions here.

ORIGINAL   _____

_____

_____

_____

_____

REVISION   _____

_____

_____

_____

_____

ORIGINAL   _____

_____

_____

_____

_____

REVISION   _____

_____

_____

_____

_____

ORIGINAL

_____

_____

_____

_____

_____

REVISION

_____

_____

_____

_____

_____

**Next, turn to the third part of this lesson
and review some basic grammar rules.**

Grammar

The subject of grammar encompasses more rules and topics than anyone can consider in one sitting. In this program, you will review the three areas of usage most likely to cause problems for business writers:

- unclear pronouns

- gender-related pronouns

- plural verbs with singular subjects (and vice versa)

PRONOUNS, CLEAR AND OTHERWISE

As you can see from these examples, unclear pronouns quickly con-fuse — and even amuse — readers.

ORIGINAL	When Marta met with Susan Garcia last week **she** agreed to accept the revised proposal.
REVISION	Susan Garcia agreed to accept the revised proposal when she met with Marta last week.
ORIGINAL	The transit officials plan to increase fares to reduce the annual deficit. **This** will be a hardship on commuters.
REVISION	Transit officials plan to increase fares to reduce the annual deficit. This increase will be a hardship on commuters.
ORIGINAL	Tom's hat didn't fit his head so he had **it** made smaller.
REVISION	Tom had his hat made smaller because it did not fit his head.

PRACTICE

See if you can clear up the confusing pronouns in these sentences. You are free to guess the writer's meaning.

1. The catalogue had a picture of the work station the company needed so Alex decided to buy it.

    _____

    _____

    _____

    _____

2. Ed was unable to finish the project on time and explained the problem to David. He was very frustrated.

    _____

    _____

    _____

    _____

Check your answers on the next page.

ANSWERS TO PRACTICE

1. Alex decided to buy the catalogue because it had a picture of the work station the company needed.

    —OR—

    Because the company needed a work station, Alex decided to buy the one pictured in the catalogue.

2. Ed was unable to finish the project on time and explained the problem to David. Ed was very frustrated.

    —OR—

    David was very frustrated when he learned Ed was unable to finish the project on time.

Using Gender-Related Pronouns

Gender refers to the way a language uses certain words to indicate masculine, feminine or neuter:

- **She** received **her** law degree in 1995.

- **His** ambition was to ride **his** bicycle across the country.

- **It's** a beautiful building.

Unlike some other languages, English does not have a singular pronoun that can refer either to males or females. Until the late 1960's, it was common practice to use masculine pronouns — **he, his, him** — to refer to either sex.

Today, however, it is no longer acceptable to use pronouns that imply you are speaking only about men when women are also represented.

GENDER-BIASED   The secretary asked **everyone** to select **his** preferred health provider option by the first of next month.

The most effective method to remove gender bias is the one shown below — revising the sentence using plural nouns and pronouns.

REVISED   The secretary asked all **employees** to select **their** preferred health provider option by the first of next month.

<u>**NOTE**</u>   It has become more acceptable to use the plural pronouns **their** and **them** with singular indefinite pronouns such as **everyone**. But when you can, try to phrase sentences to avoid gender bias without resorting to awkward constructions or poor grammar.

AWKWARD   The secretary asked **everyone** to select **his/her** preferred health provider option by the first of next month.

POOR GRAMMAR   The secretary asked **everyone** to select **their** preferred health provider option by the first of next month.

PRACTICE

See if you can revise these sentences so they are gender-free.

1. Somebody left his lights on over the weekend.

2. When compiling figures for the audit, an accountant should always make sure she has the most recent figures.

**Check your answers
on the next page**

ANSWERS TO PRACTICE

1. Lights were left on over the weekend.

2. When compiling figures for the audit, accountants should always make sure they have the most recent figures.

ASSIGNMENT

Review your own writing samples for examples of unclear pronoun references or inappropriate gender-related pronouns. If you find any, write the sentences below and then revise them. If you don't find any examples, go on to the next section of this lesson.

ORIGINAL _____

_____

_____

_____

_____

REVISION _____

_____

_____

_____

_____

ORIGINAL _____

_____

_____

_____

_____

REVISION _____

_____

_____

_____

_____

SINGULAR OR PLURAL VERBS

It's sometimes hard to know whether to use a singular verb or a plural verb, and the rules on correct usage may seem confusing.

Here are some examples. See if you can circle the letters in front of the sentences you think use the **correct** verb:

a.   Each of the systems *are* failing.

b.   Mr. Bruce and Mr. Appleby *has* received a promotion.

c.   One of the calculators *was* advertised at a thirty percent reduction.

d.   The decision of the judges *are* final.

e.   Neither of the clerks *wants* to change the hours.

You should have circled "c" and "e" because the verbs are correct.

On the next few pages you'll find rules that will help you use verbs correctly.

Words and phrases that come between a singular subject and its verb DO NOT CHANGE the number of the verb.

EXAMPLE   The **noise** of the trains **is** making me deaf.

In this case, **noise**, a singular subject, determines the verb.

Use a singular verb after certain "indefinite" pronouns.

EXAMPLE   **Each** of the systems **is** failing.

In this sentence, **each** is the "indefinite" pronoun so the verb should be singular.

Other pronouns followed by a singular verb include:

anyone	everyone
no one	somebody
everybody	either
someone	anything
everything	neither
nothing	one (of)

Two or more subjects joined by "and" take a plural verb.

EXAMPLE   Pencils **and** paper **are** required to complete the test.

In sentences that have two subjects joined by "neither-nor," "either-or," or "not only-but also," the verb agrees with the NEAREST subject.

EXAMPLE   Not only the managers but also the **president wants** to cancel the next game.

Either the coach or the **players decide** where to have dinner after the game.

If you keep these rules in mind, you should have no trouble with subject-verb agreement.

PRACTICE

Underline the correct verb in each sentence.

1. The purpose of his requests (was, were) to get the additional funds.

2. I don't think either of the boys (are, is) going to last the year.

3. Each computer, desk and printer (is, are) marked down

4. The cause of the errors (is, are) unknown.

5. One of the reasons for absences (is, are) poor health.

6. The largest of the three banks (is, are) in Petaluma.

7. Everyone I asked (agree, agrees) with my decision.

Check your answers.

ANSWERS TO PRACTICE

1. The purpose of his requests **was** to get the additional funds.

2. I don't think either of the boys **is** going to last the year.

3. Each computer, desk and printer **is** marked down.

4. The cause of the errors **is** unknown.

5. One of the reasons for absences **is** poor health.

6. The largest of the three banks **is** in Petaluma.

7. Everyone I asked **agrees** with my decision.

**There's one more practice
on the next page.**

PRACTICE

Revise these sentences so the verbs are correct. The first one is done for you.

EXAMPLE   Everybody who was in the building at the time of the fire is going to have to testify.

1. Not only the birthday girl but also her parents was amused by the juggler.

2. One of the many things she worries about are the monthly report.

3. The teachers and at least one secretary is going out on strike.

ANSWERS TO PRACTICE

1. Not only the birthday girl but also her parents **were** amused by the juggler.

2. One of the many things she worries about **is** the monthly report.

3. The teachers and at least one secretary **are** going out on strike.

ASSIGNMENT

Review your own writing samples to be sure all subjects and verbs agree. Use the space below to revise any incorrect sentences.

ORIGINAL

_____

_____

_____

_____

_____

REVISION

_____

_____

_____

_____

_____

ORIGINAL

_____

_____

_____

_____

_____

REVISION

_____

_____

_____

_____

_____

Review

To review what you've learned in this lesson, answer these questions.

1. As a general rule, keep the average length of your sentences to about _____ words, with only one or two _____ per sentence.   (165)

2. A run-on sentence contains _____ that are connected incorrectly.   (172)

3. Use a comma to set off a phrase or clause that is not _____ to the meaning of the sentence.   (185)

4. Use a semicolon to join two _____ _____ with a word such as "however," therefore," etc.   (191)

5. Words and phrases that come between a singular subject and its verb _____ _____ _____ the number of the subject.   (207)

Congratulations!

You have finished this program. If you completed all the assignments and follow all the suggestions, you should find yourself writing more clearly and with more confidence.

Turn back to the **Objectives** list on Page 3 of the Introduction. Have you achieved your objectives? If you're not sure, review the relevant section or sections of the program.

If you keep this book as a reference and keep practicing the techniques you learned, your writing will continue to improve. Before long, you'll be able to make a liar of Voltaire, who said, "God gave man [and woman] the gift of language to obscure what he [she] really means."

BIBLIOGRAPHY

MECHANICS

A *Concise Dictionary of Correct English*, B.A. Phythian, ed. A sound discussion of English grammar and an appreciation of the subtlety and variety of English expression.

Essentials of English, Vincent F. Hopper, Cedric Gale, Ronald C. Foote and Benjamin W. Griffith, Barron's. A practical grammar and handbook of effective writing techniques.

A *Manual of Style*, Chicago University Press. Comprehensive rules of usage, principles of composition, commonly misused words, etc. Particularly useful for those who write journal articles, manuals, books, etc.

The New Well-Tempered Sentence, Karen Elizabeth Gordon, Ticknor and Fields, Houghton-Mifflin Co. A punctuation handbook for the "Innocent, the Eager and the Doomed."

Pinckert's Practical Grammar, Robert C. Pinckert, Writer's Digest Books. The study of grammar, usage, punctuation and style in a "game" format.

A *Pocket Guide to Correct Punctuation*, Robert Brittain, Barron's. A quick reference for answers to questions on punctuation.

LANGUAGE

The Art of Readable Writing. Rudolf Flesch, Collier Books. Shows how to say and write what you mean in language that people understand easily.

A *Concise Dictionary of Confusables: All Those Impossible Words You Never Got Right*, B.A. Phythian, John Wiley. Helpful for making impossible words more possible.

The Goof-Proofer, Stephen J. Manhard, MacMillan. A sure-fire way to improve your speaking and writing.

BIBLIOGRAPHY, Continued

WRITING

The Elements of Style, William Strunk, Jr. and E.B. White, MacMillan Company. Includes rules of usage, principles of composition, and a list of commonly misused words and expressions.

Essentials of Writing, Vincent F. Hopper, Barron's. A graduated series of exercises in basic writing techniques.

How to Write: Communicating Ideas and Information, Herbert E. Meyer and Jill M. Meyer, Storm King Press. A step-by-step process for writing anything — even thank-you notes.

Write Right!, Jan Venolia, Ten Speed Press. A handy first-aid kit and preventive maintenance manual for the written word.

Writing with Power: Techniques for Mastering the Writing Process, Peter Elbow, Oxford University Press. Method for getting power over yourself and over the writing process; knowing what you really mean; and writing convincingly.

REMOVING WRITER'S BLOCK

Writing Down the Bones: Freeing the Writer Within, Natalie Goldberg, Shambhala Publications, Inc. Thoughts, suggestions, encouragement and exercises that help free your creativity and allow your ideas to flow unencumbered onto the page.

Writing on Both Sides of the Brain, Henriette Anne Klauser, Harper S.F. Based on the premise that writing and editing are two separate brain functions. Provides techniques for freeing the creative side and methods for honing editing skills.

Writing the Natural Way — Using Right-Brain Techniques, Gabriele Cresser Rico, J.P. Tarcher. "Right-brain" techniques, including "clustering," that increase spontaneity and creativity in your writing.

WRITING WORKSHEET

SUBJECT: _____

1. LOOK AT WHAT YOU'RE GOING TO WRITE FROM YOUR **READER'S** POINT OF VIEW.

   Name or describe reader(s): _____

   Write 5 - 6 points to keep in mind about your reader(s):

   _____

   _____

   _____

   _____

   _____

   _____

2. DECIDE ON YOUR **PRIMARY** PURPOSE:

   ☐ INFLUENCE   ☐ INFORM

3. COMPOSE A **KEY SENTENCE:**

   I want my reader(s) to do or to know:

   _____

   _____

   _____

   _____

   _____

   _____

4. LIST THE **FACTS AND IDEAS** TO INCLUDE:

_____	_____
_____	_____
_____	_____
_____	_____
_____	_____
_____	_____

Continue on another page if necessary.

5. GROUP POINTS INTO **CATEGORIES** (Key points):

_____	_____
_____	_____
_____	_____
_____	_____

6. WRITE A **SUMMARY SENTENCE** FOR EACH CATEGORY AND PUT THEM IN ORDER:

_____

_____

_____

_____

_____

_____

_____

Continue on another page if necessary.

WRITING WORKSHEET

SUBJECT: _____

1. LOOK AT WHAT YOU'RE GOING TO WRITE FROM YOUR **READER'S** POINT OF VIEW.

   Name or describe reader(s): _____

   Write 5 - 6 points to keep in mind about your reader(s):

   _____

   _____

   _____

   _____

   _____

   _____

   _____

2. DECIDE ON YOUR **PRIMARY** PURPOSE:

   ☐ INFLUENCE   ☐ INFORM

3. COMPOSE A **KEY SENTENCE:**

   I want my reader(s) to do or to know:

   _____

   _____

   _____

   _____

   _____

   _____

4. LIST THE **FACTS AND IDEAS** TO INCLUDE:

_____   _____

_____   _____

_____   _____

_____   _____

_____   _____

_____   _____

_____   _____

Continue on another page if necessary.

5. GROUP POINTS INTO **CATEGORIES** (Key points):

_____   _____

_____   _____

_____   _____

_____   _____

6. WRITE A **SUMMARY SENTENCE** FOR EACH CATEGORY AND PUT THEM IN ORDER:

_____

_____

_____

_____

_____

_____

Continue on another page if necessary.

WRITING WORKSHEET

SUBJECT: _____

1. LOOK AT WHAT YOU'RE GOING TO WRITE FROM YOUR
   READER'S POINT OF VIEW.

   Name or describe reader(s): _____

   Write 5 - 6 points to keep in mind about your reader(s):

   _____

   _____

   _____

   _____

   _____

   _____

2. DECIDE ON YOUR **PRIMARY** PURPOSE:

   ☐ INFLUENCE   ☐ INFORM

3. COMPOSE A **KEY SENTENCE:**

   I want my reader(s) to do or to know:

   _____

   _____

   _____

   _____

   _____

   _____

4. LIST THE **FACTS AND IDEAS** TO INCLUDE:

_____   _____
_____   _____
_____   _____
_____   _____
_____   _____
_____   _____
_____   _____

Continue on another page if necessary.

5. GROUP POINTS INTO **CATEGORIES** (Key points):

_____   _____
_____   _____
_____   _____
_____   _____
_____   _____

6. WRITE A **SUMMARY SENTENCE** FOR EACH CATEGORY AND PUT THEM IN ORDER:

_____
_____
_____
_____
_____
_____
_____

Continue on another page if necessary.

WRITING WORKSHEET

SUBJECT: _____

1. LOOK AT WHAT YOU'RE GOING TO WRITE FROM YOUR **READER'S** POINT OF VIEW.

   Name or describe reader(s): _____

   Write 5 - 6 points to keep in mind about your reader(s):

   _____

   _____

   _____

   _____

   _____

   _____

   _____

2. DECIDE ON YOUR **PRIMARY** PURPOSE:

   ☐ INFLUENCE   ☐ INFORM

3. COMPOSE A **KEY SENTENCE:**

   I want my reader(s) to do or to know:

   _____

   _____

   _____

   _____

   _____

   _____

4. LIST THE **FACTS AND IDEAS** TO INCLUDE:

_____   _____

_____   _____

_____   _____

_____   _____

_____   _____

_____   _____

_____   _____

Continue on another page if necessary.

5. GROUP POINTS INTO **CATEGORIES** (Key points):

_____   _____

_____   _____

_____   _____

_____   _____

_____   _____

6. WRITE A **SUMMARY SENTENCE** FOR EACH CATEGORY AND PUT THEM IN ORDER:

_____

_____

_____

_____

_____

_____

Continue on another page if necessary.

WRITING WORKSHEET

SUBJECT: _____

1. LOOK AT WHAT YOU'RE GOING TO WRITE FROM YOUR
    READER'S POINT OF VIEW.

    Name or describe reader(s): _____

    Write 5 - 6 points to keep in mind about your reader(s):

    _____

    _____

    _____

    _____

    _____

    _____

    _____

2. DECIDE ON YOUR **PRIMARY** PURPOSE:

    ☐ INFLUENCE   ☐ INFORM

3. COMPOSE A **KEY SENTENCE:**

    I want my reader(s) to do or to know:

    _____

    _____

    _____

    _____

    _____

    _____

4. LIST THE **FACTS AND IDEAS** TO INCLUDE:

_____   _____

_____   _____

_____   _____

_____   _____

_____   _____

_____   _____

_____   _____

Continue on another page if necessary.

5. GROUP POINTS INTO **CATEGORIES** (Key points):

_____   _____

_____   _____

_____   _____

_____   _____

_____   _____

6. WRITE A **SUMMARY SENTENCE** FOR EACH CATEGORY AND PUT THEM IN ORDER:

_____

_____

_____

_____

_____

_____

Continue on another page if necessary.